THE
PSYCHOPATH

ALSO BY MARY TURNER THOMSON

The Bigamist

THE
PSYCHOPATH

A TRUE STORY

Mary Turner Thomson

Published by Little A, Seattle

www.apub.com

Amazon, the Amazon logo, and Little A are trademarks of Amazon.com,
Inc., or its affiliates.

ISBN-13: 9781542024990 (paperback)
ISBN-10: 1542024994 (paperback)

ISBN-13: 9781542028714 (hardback)
ISBN-10: 154202871X (hardback)

Cover design by The Brewster Project

Cover photo courtesy of the author

Printed in the United States of America

For my children,
who inspired me to live my best life
and to not only weather the storm but to
rise from the ashes and build a better world

AUTHOR'S NOTE

This is a true account as I remember it, and as it has been told to me by other victims of Will Jordan. Many of the names have been changed to protect those who do not want to be identified. I have used my own name because I have never felt that I have anything to hide and I feel very strongly that by standing up to talk about this issue I am helping others to speak out as well. I have used Will Jordan's real name because I feel it is important to protect past and potential future victims who may not know who he is, and by using his name they may find some peace in finally knowing the truth.

When my first book, *The Bigamist*, was originally published, I didn't use my children's real names because they were too young to decide for themselves whether they were content to be identified. However, as my children grew up, they were annoyed with me because they don't feel they have anything to hide either. So in the latest edition their real names are used: Robyn, Eilidh and Zach, as they are here.

I also invented the name 'Michele' for Will Jordan's other British wife in my previous book, to protect her privacy. However, one of the newer victims is called 'Mischele', something which might cause confusion and indeed it has confused the press on occasion. Mischele (the newer victim) wants me to use her real name. I have therefore not used a name for Will Jordan's other British wife when referred to in this book. I suppose, due to the number of women involved in this extraordinary story, it was not surprising that names would be duplicated!

PROLOGUE

I was numb. I hovered in the carnage that was my life like a movie scene from the aftermath of a bomb attack. Ears ringing and deaf to the chaos around me as everything exploded outwards. My external world shattered as my mind inside crumbled. At that moment I could not imagine how anything would ever be 'all right' again. The devastation was all-consuming and left me wondering how it would even be possible to recover at all. But recover I have.

In 2006, I lost everything from the life I knew. It had all been taken from me by the man I'd fallen in love with in 2000 and married (bigamously as it turned out) in 2002. My savings and everything I had built up financially as an adult had disappeared; work was gone and with it my ability to earn money; my home was taken away, leaving my children and me to the mercy and whims of a landlord; the debts incurred in my name were astronomical. The man whom I had pledged 'to have and to hold' had turned out to be a monster who not only impregnated women to rip them off for money but psychologically tortured and abused women all his life – mentally, emotionally and financially crippling them just for his own amusement. This man who had professed to be my soulmate had got into my head and systematically changed my thinking, making me live in fear and robbing me of my powers of expression, keeping me silent so I couldn't articulate what was happening to me. He made me love him whilst he was abusing me.

I had given everything to this man, my body, my heart, my money, my voice and my mind – but I had been sleeping with the enemy. I had been fooled, manipulated, conned, abused – emotionally crumpled up like a piece of rubbish and discarded. My self-confidence and my self-esteem were shattered.

I kept asking myself, 'How could I have been so completely taken in by this consummate liar?' And it threatened to silence me all over again because I knew others were also asking the same question. How could I have been so stupid, desperate, needy or naive?

However, the far more important question was, 'Where do I go from here?'

I still had something to help me hold it all together though. My children. Robyn, Eilidh and Zach. No matter what had happened I still had them, and I owed it to them to find a way out of the quagmire.

Spoiler alert, I not only moved forward but I found my voice and used it to climb out of the pit and up a mountain. I not only made it back, I created a new and more vibrant life for myself and my family. When I finished writing *The Bigamist* I was still breathing. I was surviving after my traumatic experience. Now, as I finish writing *The Psychopath*, I feel lucky and grateful to be where I am. Not grateful to my abuser, but thankful to have had the opportunity to test my mettle and use my experiences to help others. I have not only recovered, I've become immune to toxic personalities, and now use my knowledge to show people who are in a similar situation how to escape, survive and thrive, through my writing and speaking.

This book is about my journey to the top of that seemingly overwhelmingly high mountain and proof that recovery from a psychopath is possible. It is also the story of what that psychopath did next.

THE END

My life changed forever on 5 April 2006 when I answered the phone and the woman on the other end introduced herself as my husband's other wife. Suddenly, the walls of my terrifying world crumbled around me and I was free from the abuse and control that I wasn't even aware had trapped me. I look back on that moment now with even more clarity as time gives me the wisdom to see what was really happening.

For a while in 2006 I seemed to be living my life in a vacuum. I functioned, and as the days turned into weeks I gradually stopped having to remind myself to breathe in and out – but I could still only focus on one thing at a time. I would take my children to school and I got my son a free nursery place for a few hours a day. When he was there, I would go and see my mother and busy myself helping her. I concentrated on each task in turn because it stopped me from thinking about what I had just come through and the wider situation I was in.

I got a lot of support from the health visitor who had recommended the nursery place as well as pointing me in the direction of other organisations who could help. When Will Jordan, who was still my husband at that stage, was first taken to court for a preliminary hearing in April 2006, there was a lot of media interest. The crime of bigamy is quite rare in itself, and the addition of fraud, firearms offences and failure to register under the Sexual Offences Act made it a particularly juicy story for the press. Everywhere I went I took the newspaper articles with me because I was convinced people wouldn't believe me when I told them what had happened. I was surprised when people just automatically assumed I was telling the truth and didn't immediately ask to see the evidence. I put a brave face on things and told everyone I was fine, but really I was in a perpetual state of limbo, shuttling between shock and panic.

I held my children close and talked to them gently. My four-year-old daughter, Eilidh, used to sit on my lap and cry her heart out and I cried with her as I rocked her and we grieved the loss of our family unit together. Robyn, my seven-year-old, was less demonstrative and pushed the emotions down. She would cuddle me and she talked openly about it but didn't cry as much. My son, who was only a year old, didn't really know what was going on. It was all I could do to try and keep life as normal as I could for them.

I couldn't work though. I couldn't focus on anything else other than putting one foot in front of another. I had to register for benefits to survive financially. I was signed off on state-funded incapacity benefit or 'sick pay', which is usually reviewed on a regular basis to ensure you're not scamming the system. I was called to a medical review after a couple of months and as usual I took the articles with me. I went into the doctor's office and showed them to her. She commented that I was holding it together very well and signed me off indefinitely. I am still very grateful for that – particularly in the first year, when I had nothing and had hit rock bottom.

Once I had found my voice and started to talk to people, I found that I couldn't stop. I had been kept silent long enough, and felt compelled to tell people about it. I told everyone I spoke to about what had happened. Not in intricate detail but I would spill out the gist before I even knew I was talking about it again. My friends were very patient with me, but I knew that eventually it would start to grate and tried hard to stop talking about it to them. Then I started to tell strangers instead, anyone that I hadn't already banged on to about the subject. It got so I had to consciously stop myself from talking about it. I would be standing at a bus stop and someone would say, 'Good morning' to me – something that is quite common still in Scotland. I would smile and reply, 'Good morning' and then add, 'I've just found out my husband is a bigamist and a con man.' It was almost like I was rebelling against the years of silence and having been told I couldn't tell anyone anything at all. Sometimes they would react with shock and avoid any further conversation, but sometimes they were fascinated and engage in conversation, which helped me gradually make sense of what had happened.

I also had a compulsion to find out more, to talk to other victims of Will Jordan and understand the bigger picture. I was in regular contact with Alice Kean, the woman who had been his 'employee', who had been engaged to him and defrauded by him. He had used her credit card to pay for repairs to his car and she had set up a police sting to catch him. Between us we found George, Will Jordan's son in the USA, who introduced me to his mother Devi who had been Will Jordan's childhood sweetheart when he was fifteen and she was fourteen years old. My husband's other wife in the UK had told me about Will Jordan's first wife in the USA, Alexis, and it was not too difficult to track her down. Alexis had married Will Jordan when he was twenty-three years old and he had defrauded her of money as well as cheated on her with both Devi and the woman who was later to become his wife in the UK.

I requested itemised mobile phone bills and went through the numbers. There I found businesses that Will Jordan had defrauded, including a man called Malcolm who told me he had been conned too. Malcolm also told me about the numerous other business people he had been in contact with when he'd investigated Will Jordan himself.

Each of the victims I tracked down and talked to added to the picture and it became clearer that this was a lifelong pattern of behaviour. The more people I talked to, the more victims I found – the bigger picture was huge.

In the summer of 2006 I wanted to read about how other people had dealt with similar situations, so at some point I walked into a bookshop and asked for a book about bigamy or being conned by a lover, telling the assistant briefly what had happened to me. He shrugged, looking astonished, and said he didn't know of anything like that.

I have been an avid reader since my early 20s and usually read novels, but I found after April 2006 that I couldn't read anything except true crime. For nearly a year I only read stories about domestic violence, child abuse and tales of survival in traumatic situations. I had admired Alice Sebold's novel *The Lovely Bones* in 2004 and came across her memoir *Lucky*, which is the story of her own horrific rape and how she recovered from it – more than that, it was how her rape had affected everyone around her and I could see where the story of *The Lovely Bones* had come from. Something she said really resonated with me though. She talked about PTSD and how she had surrounded herself with violence to make her own past feel more normal. I realised that I was surrounding myself with horrific stories of abuse, manipulation and coercive control too. It helped normalise my own situation and made me feel less alone. However, there was nothing out there that truly matched what I had been through. Surely I was not the only one?

My mother helped me hold my head above water with her sympathetic, matter-of-fact, calm strength. Even after finding out that she was losing her battle with Non-Hodgkin's lymphoma (just weeks after discovering my husband was a bigamist), she was there for me. She was amazingly supportive throughout the last four months, helping me recover whilst I helped her with shopping and cooking, etc. I spent as much time with her as possible whilst she fought her cancer.

She told me to stand tall and to write my story down. She knew my experience could help other people and that telling it would help me. She told me that there must be others who had been through similar situations but if people weren't talking about it then maybe I should.

The last time I saw my mum was in hospital on 14 August 2006. She was tired and uncomfortable. She was ready to let go but still had her sense of humour. The nurse asked her if she needed anything.

My mum replied, 'Yes, a big rock!'

The nurse looked confused, so I added calmly, 'It's to hit her over the head with.'

'Ah, I see,' said the nurse. 'I don't think I have one of those.'

Mum didn't like to make a fuss but she was in a lot of pain and struggling to breathe. It was hard to see her in so much discomfort, so I told her to make sure that she asked for more morphine if she needed it. At that stage the hospital knew it was only a matter of time until she died and they were just trying to make her as comfortable as possible. I knew that visit was probably the last time I would see her and tried not to show her how sad I was, even though my heart was breaking all over again. We talked about writing my book, and she told me she had no concerns about me at all. She said, 'I want you to have my wedding ring. I've had some good years out of it, forty-nine to be precise, so I hope it will see you happy too. And Mary, keep at it – it's all going to work out for you.'

I didn't want to leave her that night and thought about sleeping in the chair by her side but she told me she was tired and I had to go home to my children. So I left her with a notebook of mine so she could write things down if she wanted to. I hugged her and told her I loved her, then said I would see her tomorrow, knowing in my heart that I might not but at the time selfishly hoping we could have at least one more day together.

When it became obvious early the next morning that she only had a short time left, the nurses wanted to call us back in but Mum told them not to. She didn't want us to bear the distress of seeing her die. So the nurses only called us at the very last minute and by the time we arrived it was too late. Mum died on the morning of 15 August 2006.

A week later, on 22 August 2006, we held a celebration of my mother's life with a humanist ceremony at Mortonhall Crematorium. We had to move the celebration from the small chapel to the big chapel because so many people said they were coming.

Professionally she was an interior designer but she had also been a campaigner for the arts, a hostess of wonderful parties, and a collector of lost souls. She had touched many lives and made them all better. Amongst various other things she had sat on the Art in Architecture awards panel for the Saltire Society and travelled all around Scotland looking at buildings and showing appreciation for them. She absolutely hated the Mortonhall Crematorium building and had said on many occasions that if she could, she would knock it down and start over. However we had no other choice of venue so the celebration of her life as well as the cremation were held there.

It was a beautiful summer day and I stood outside the crematorium with my father and three older siblings waiting for people to arrive, feeling like my chest was being ripped open. It was suffocating. More and more people arrived, and as per her wishes, everyone wore lots of colours as a mark of respect. It was overwhelming: 150 brightly clad people, each saying what an amazing woman my mother was and how much they had appreciated having her in their lives. She had been such a bright light to so many people and it helped to know her life had had such meaning.

I don't remember the service at all, though I know it was positive and validating that so many people loved her and wanted to be there. I believe that my brother and eldest sister spoke but I have no recollection of it. I think I was just trying to hold myself together and keep from dissolving into a puddle. Even now, I can't think of her without my chest burning and big fat tears rolling down my cheeks.

In line with Mum's request we had a party back at her house afterwards with champagne and smoked salmon. Everyone had a story to tell about her – about how she had helped them, how she had inspired them, how her life had meant so much to so many people. It truly was a celebration of her life, just as she had wanted.

The next day I listened to the news and fell about laughing, probably the first time I had laughed since she died. There had been a fire at Mortonhall Crematorium shortly after we had left. The door to the crematorium had not been closed properly and it had set fire to the roof. It had taken five fire engines and twenty-five firefighters nearly six hours to put out the blaze. Thankfully no one was hurt. I called the crematorium and asked if it had been my mother's cremation that had set off the fire and the telephone operator nervously told me, 'No, no, there were no human remains in the cremation chamber when the fire started.'

'Why on earth was the cremator lit then?' I asked.

I just got a rather short and mumbled reply and then they quickly hung up.

My mother didn't believe in life after death, but if there'd been one thing she could do it would have been to burn down that building, so to me it was utterly delightful that the fire at the crematorium had happened on that day. Also it was something that Mum would have found highly amusing.

THE PURGE

As per Mum's wishes, and only two days after she died, I attended my first writing workshop at the Edinburgh Book Festival. The day after her funeral I went to the second of the workshops. It was a creative writing session attended by about twenty people, all sitting in a circle with notebooks in hand. The first exercise we had to do was to tell the others three things that had happened to us recently that we could write a story about. Each person said their piece and then it came to me.

'Well, in April I found out my husband was a bigamist and a con man who actively impregnates women to rip them off for money; last week my mum died; and yesterday she set fire to Mortonhall Crematorium after her funeral.'

As you can imagine, the reaction was rather like I had set off a small explosion in the centre of the group and their shocked faces made me laugh out loud. I must have looked totally insane.

Then the next person said, 'How on earth can I follow that?'

The third session I attended was a 'Life Writing' discussion, in which the literary agent Jenny Brown talked to a publisher about the sort of work they commissioned. During the session I asked a question and at the end I leapt out of my seat to catch the presenters before they left the theatre. I blurted out a quick summary of my story and they both gave me their cards asking to meet me for a further chat.

I met with Jenny Brown in a little café just near her offices. We sat down and I explained in detail what had happened. Jenny was brilliant and very encouraging. At first she said that I would need a ghostwriter as I had never written or published anything before but I explained that I wanted to tell the story in my own words and use any book I created to start a new life. She suggested I send her a chapter to see what she thought and her response when I did was lovely. She wrote, 'Well, the one thing that is clear is that you don't need a ghostwriter!' It was very encouraging and boosted my confidence enormously.

The first publishers I met were bowled over by the story as well. We had one meeting and they offered me an advance. I found that fascinating – I was a complete unknown, and they had no idea if I could write, but the story was so extraordinary that it warranted paying me an advance to see if I could produce a book! If my mother could have been anything she wanted, she would have been an author, and for me to get a publishing deal only a month after she had died felt like honouring her. I was deeply sad that she was not alive to see that happen but I did feel that I was doing her proud.

So finally I set about putting down on paper what had happened and how. It was difficult to start with because all the thoughts would tumble and rush about in my head. It was like trying to find the end of a huge ball of tightly knotted spaghetti in my mind. There was too much noise and confusion. So I wrote the most recent and dramatic thing first – the phone call from the other wife and meeting her. Doing that freed up some space in my head, and loosened the knot. It let me find the end of another part of the story.

I got up every morning at 5 a.m. and wrote for two hours before the kids woke up. I got them up, breakfasted and off to school and nursery. Then I would go to a café for a few hours and write, pouring everything out into notebooks that I carried around with me everywhere.

That tangled ball of spaghetti in my head started to unravel and with each chapter I could see the situation more clearly. Each time I found the end of a thought and started to write it down it was like the spaghetti became words and lines on the page. Writing ordered the thoughts that had swirled around my befuddled head for years, solidifying them into something tangible – like Dumbledore, magically pulling memories out of my head and transferring them to a 'pensieve', Dumbledore's magic basin for holding memories and thoughts, to free up space. It was a proactive healing process and incredibly cathartic. The more I wrote, the faster and more urgent the writing became, like I was purging the whole experience from my mind.

It took me just three months to write the first draft of the whole book because I was so driven to release it. Afterwards I felt liberated.

I had taken the first step and reclaimed my mind. That area of my life, my thought processes, were mine again and I was back in the driving seat. There was still a long road to full recovery but mentally I was now stronger and more in control.

Writing it down brought up questions though. Why had Will Jordan done what he had done? What reasons did he have for choosing me? And, more importantly, what made me vulnerable to him? I could see his actions and the reality of what my situation had been with more clarity after writing it down, but I couldn't make sense of the 'how' or the 'why'.

I have always believed in personal responsibility – a simple concept of looking at any situation from the perspective of your own actions. Put simply, you can't change the past but you can learn from it; you also can't change other people, but you can change yourself, and thereby affect how others around you act. Being personally responsible means choosing the ability to respond to any given situation based on your own actions. But that meant looking at *my* own actions and analysing what *I* had done (or not done) that had caused this to happen to me. What was it about me that showed Will Jordan that I was a target? How was it that I was so taken in by his charm that my natural defences were not raised, and I fell heavily in love, letting him into my head? What could I learn that would ensure I would never be victimised by someone like him again?

I didn't just want to tell my story, I wanted to understand why it had happened at all. So at the same time as writing *The Bigamist*, I started to research people like him. What I found out was fascinating!

THE PSYCHOPATH

At first, it was hard to find out more about people like Will Jordan because I didn't have the language to know what questions to ask. There was very little online about bigamy other than to describe what it was in legal terms. I searched terms like 'liar' and 'fraud' but nothing came close to the situation I had been in. Then I asked a question about manipulation and abuse in relationships and came across a website – www.lovefraud.com – set up and run by Donna Anderson. It was a revelation. Suddenly here was a whole community of people who had experienced something similar to me. Here was a website dedicated to recovering and sharing stories like mine. I read article after article about people being victimised by emotionless predators and it sounded all too familiar. I devoured the site hour after hour, soaking in all the information like a starving child being given a first meal. Suddenly I was no longer alone and the first piece of the puzzle fell into place.

Donna had been the victim of a sociopath, and launched her website in 2005 to help protect others from being exploited in the same way. I wrote to Donna telling her what had happened to me and she was incredibly supportive. I had found a community of people who truly understood what I had been through because they had experienced something similar. I now had a name for what he was – a sociopath. It gave me the starting point I needed to find out more.

As I delved further into the research I discovered that sociopaths and psychopaths are essentially the same thing, but with one crucial difference. Psychopaths are born, and sociopaths are made.

From my understanding of the research reports I have read, a psychopath is born without any chemical empathic response and therefore has no emotion or ability to love. Basically, if I deliberately broke my finger in front of you with a loud 'snap' you are likely to wince, your eyes crinkle, duck your head down or back with a sharp intake of breath. That is because empathic people have a chemical empathic response to other people's pain. It lights up parts of our brains which make us 'feel' other people's pain inside our own heads, like a hot needle being seared into our brains. Psychopaths are born without that. The lack of that simple chemical response changes everything: no empathy means no love, no remorse, no guilt, no shame. Without empathy there is no emotional connection to other people and no internal restrictions on what one person can do to another.

Unlike a psychopath, a sociopath might be born with 'chemical empathic response', but due to early childhood abuse and neglect has it conditioned out of them, and as a result grows up without empathy for others.

Neither 'psychopath' nor 'sociopath' are official titles in medical terms, nor are they listed in the Diagnostic and Statistical Manual of Mental Disorders (the current version is DSM5), which is the definitive book on what is and is not classed as a mental disorder in the international psychiatric community. Both these terms (along with narcissism) come under the DSM5 category of 'Antisocial Personality Disorder'. Because they aren't official terms, there is a lot of variation in the research articles about the finer details of the individual personality disorders, so this is just an overall layman's perspective on the information I've gleaned.

The words themselves tell you which is which – 'Psych' meaning to do with the brain/mind itself, 'Socio' meaning to do with society, and 'path' meaning a diseased or suffering person. From the articles I read it appears that once an individual grows up, the conditions are indistinguishable from each other, so I will use the term 'psychopath' to cover both. I initially thought Will Jordan was a sociopath but over the years the definitions have changed and I later realised it's more likely that he is a psychopath.

Psychopaths are not mentally ill – they are quite rational and in control – in some sense far more so than neurotypical or empathic people. Psychopathy is a personality disorder characterised by persistent antisocial behaviour by someone with impaired empathy and remorse, demonstrating bold, disinhibited and egotistical traits. It is generally considered incurable and untreatable because it involves a lack of chemical response – something that can be suppressed pharmaceutically but cannot be recreated with drugs or therapy. In any case, a psychopath, by definition, wouldn't seek treatment even if it was available. (As a side note, if you have ever worried if you might be a psychopath then that's proof you're not – a psychopath would never worry about it.)

Due to their lack of concern for anyone, people around them become like characters in the video game *The Sims*: to be used, played with and discarded at will. They have learnt techniques through repetition of this game that help them seduce their victims. Two of the techniques I started to see mentioned repeatedly on sites that I visited are love-bombing and gaslighting – both of which are toxic methods of controlling people. Reading up on them gave me absolute clarity that this is what Will Jordan had done to me.

'Love-bombing' starts with compliments, endearing gestures and public displays of affection, constant and intimate messages, and lavish gifts. They will refer to being 'soulmates' and declare undying love within a few weeks of meeting and generally it feels like they're pulling the relationship forward a little too fast, but the targeted individual goes with it to see where it leads. Basically, psychopaths demonstrate a level of commitment which is out of proportion to the length of time that the couple have known each other. They'll provide anything that someone might want from the perfect blossoming romance and the sort of things you see in romantic movies as the couple are swept off their feet in love. Most importantly, it will be everything that the target will be most impressed by and feel emotionally connected to.

As a single mother with an optimistic outlook, most addictive for me was the promise of a better future for me and my one-year-old daughter Robyn. Will Jordan spent time at the beginning of the relationship finding out about my desires and goals, making sure to reflect those back to me, to show that being with him would far exceed my expectations. He encouraged me to think bigger and further outside my comfort zone, thereby putting me off balance whilst also encouraging me to believe that this new partner only had my best interests at heart. This all sounds delightful and indeed would have been had it not all been done to suck me under his control. It is a conscious and deliberate act on the part of a psychopath. 'Love-bombing' has nothing to do with love. It is a calculating, unemotional tactic designed to hook you in and keep you there. I was not being put on a pedestal, I was being glued to it.

Love-bombing doesn't last forever though. Once the target is addicted to the relationship, the toxic partner will gradually switch to 'gaslighting' – a term that was coined after the 1944 film *Gaslight*, in which the husband purposefully makes his wife think she is going mad in order to hide his criminal activity. The person who had been affectionate and attentive now becomes controlling and little by little makes their partner question their own reality. Anyone is susceptible to gaslighting, and it's a common technique of abusers, dictators, and cult leaders. Gaslighting is done slowly and involves brainwashing the victim to the point that they feel they are losing their mind.

Will Jordan did this from the very beginning – before I had even met him. When we started talking online he sent me long flowing emails about his past and about the person he was. We wrote back and forth and I told him my dreams and aspirations as well as other very personal things. We wrote three, four, five times a day and never ran out of things to say. It became intoxicating and even though I tried to keep myself grounded, I was being swept away by the romance of it. Then we agreed to talk on the phone for the first time. He asked for my number and I gave it to him, and he said he would call within half an hour. I waited for the phone to ring. As the time stretched on, I went through a kaleidoscope of emotions – nervous about talking to him for the first time, anticipating the potential relationship, then confusion as to why he hadn't called. I got angry, then felt foolish thinking maybe I had misunderstood what he meant. I checked his email to see what he had said about calling, and checked mine in case I had given him the wrong number. It had all been crystal clear. The number had been correct and the time agreed. What's more, he had been incredibly enthusiastic about calling. I emailed him to ask what had happened but there was nothing back – when he would normally respond almost immediately. I worried that he had had an accident, wondered whether it had all been a joke to him, and even if I had imagined it all!

The truth was he had set the whole thing up just so I would go through that array of emotions. It was gaslighting. When he got in touch two days later with an excuse about his work taking him away to Spain, I told him to get lost. Then the love-bombing started again and gradually I was sucked back in.

◆ ◆ ◆

Even as I was learning all this, I was finding it hard to comprehend. Could I really have been in the clutches of a psychopath? My understanding of the condition was purely from cold-blooded murderers like Ted Bundy, Jeffrey Dahmer and John Wayne Gacy, or movies such as *Silence of the Lambs*. Surely such people were exceedingly rare.

Through my research I came across Dr Robert Hare, a Canadian psychologist known for his work in the field of criminal psychology and considered to be one of the world's leading experts on psychopathy. I read his book *Without Conscience: The Disturbing World of the Psychopaths Among Us*, which contained this description:

Individuals with this personality disorder are fully aware of the consequences of their actions and know the difference between right and wrong, yet they are terrifyingly self-centered, remorseless, and unable to care about the feelings of others. Perhaps most frightening, they often seem completely normal to unsuspecting targets – and they do not always ply their trade by killing.

I started to read everything I could about psychopaths and the more I read, the more familiar the diagnosis became, but I still couldn't accept that the man who had stroked my hair so tenderly and gazed into my eyes as he declared his undying devotion could indeed be so cold. This was the father of my two youngest children, the man I had believed to be my soulmate, my lover, my friend and my husband. It was a huge shift to accept that none of it had been real.

Then I discovered Dr Hare's 'Psychopathy Checklist – Revised' (PCL-R) – a test that is recognised worldwide, and used in psychiatric facilities to define whether or not someone is indeed a 'psychopath'. It is also used to determine predicted risk for criminal reoffending and probability of rehabilitation. It was the piece of information that changed everything for me.

Dr Hare initially developed the test in the 1970s developing previous research work done by Hervey Cleckley (author of *The Mask of Sanity*) in the 1940s.

The PCL-R test is a psychological assessment tool and should only really be administered by a qualified professional clinician under scientifically controlled and licensed standardised conditions. However, reading through the test was like looking through a checklist of the last six years of my life and another piece of the puzzle snapped resoundingly into place.

The Psychopath Test

The questions in the PCL-R are scored on a three-point structure: either as 0 (for not at all), 1 (for somewhat) and 2 (for definitely). A maximum score of 40 is possible from the 20 statements. Anything above 25 in the UK and 30 in the USA classes the person tested as a 'psychopath' (although this benchmark changes depending on the source). Anyone getting towards 40 would be classed as 'highly psychopathic'; this is quite rare as they have to show all of the main qualities across 20 areas of functioning. Had I asked any of these questions about Will Jordan when I first met him he would have got zero points because I didn't know the truth. But by now, I had a much better understanding of the bigger picture, so I went through the checklist point by point and this is what I found.

Glib and superficial charm

I remembered the first time I met Will Jordan in his plush Edinburgh offices – the easy way with which he walked towards me, his eyes twinkling, his hand outstretched and his huge warm smile. He never came across as arrogant or brash, always just calmly charming. Every time I introduced him to my friends or family they found him interesting and intelligent – there was often something they couldn't quite put their finger on but he came across as harmless.

The definition of 'glib' is 'fluent but insincere and shallow'. I thought about the very first emails that Will Jordan sent me – before we even met. How he seemed to be opening up to me and revealing his insecurities around being infertile due to a bout of mumps as a child. It was his 'baggage', as he put it, but he was dealing with it. He talked at length and easily about his coming to terms with not being able to father children as well as having focused heavily on his career because of it. And it felt good to have a man talk to me so openly about his feelings. His infertility made him that much more of a suitable prospect for me as I already had a child and wanted Robyn to have a father figure in her life – someone who would truly love her as his own. It was all easy, and it was all totally insincere. Outright lies, in fact. Whilst he was writing that first email about being infertile, not only did he already have at least six children, but both his wife, and his wife's nanny, were pregnant by him at the time.

Score: 2

Grandiose estimation of self

The first thing that came to mind with regards to grandiosity was the time that Will Jordan and I walked into a hotel and went up to the reception desk to check in. The receptionist referred to him as 'Dr Jordan', to which he replied, 'Mr is fine.'

I was surprised and rather confused – I'd been married to him for over a year and it had never been mentioned before. In the lift going up to the room I quizzed him about it. He didn't want to talk about it but I didn't let up and eventually he explained he had got a PhD in information technology in the early 1990s in the emerging world of computing. He didn't use the title because the field had moved so fast since then that his knowledge had been far exceeded by other people with lesser titles. He explained that because an administrator had booked the hotel room they had used his official title in error.

Looking back I can see that whole situation was set up – just so we could have that conversation. He came across as humble rather than arrogant but often subtly demonstrated a grandiose sense of himself. For instance he said that he had a black belt in karate and demonstrated kicks – he even mentioned to me that his mother had tried to get him into a martial arts movie when he was eighteen and she still had the videos of his 'try-out' – she offered to send them to me via email but I never received them. Indeed, I suspect the emails I received from her were actually Will Jordan just pretending to be his mother.

Score: 2

Need for stimulation (prone to boredom)

As I read about psychopaths needing stimulation and being prone to boredom I thought about the day when, on holiday, I found a wedding ring placed on the neatly made bed. It wasn't mine, nor was it the one I had given him. Will Jordan had left earlier to go to a meeting and was due back that night. Things had been going well for us as a family and for once everything seemed calm and settled. Then this ring appeared, and it prompted me to look in the briefcase Will Jordan had left behind – something he never did! I felt like I was betraying his trust, but the wedding band on the bed had fuelled an insatiable desire to know more. When I opened the bag I found children's passports and a wedding certificate between Will Jordan and another woman dated 1992 – ten years before my marriage to him. I immediately phoned him and he came home to explain that this was all his cover story, the certificate was faked and the children looked nothing like him – he explained that they weren't even remotely mixed race.

I realise now that the whole incident was engineered just to push the boundaries, to up the game. When things were going too smoothly, it was boring to him. He wanted to make it more exciting because pulling it all back from the flames was what he enjoyed. He needed the stimulation that risking everything created.

It also occurred to me that this was why he moved from job to job. His work with a large software company was incredibly lucrative – he was earning around £10,000 per month – but he didn't even try to do the work he was being paid for. He just billed them and produced shoddy half measures because the work was simply not stimulating enough.

Score: 2

Pathological lying

From the very first email Will Jordan had lied to me about his marital status, his name, his background and his infertility. Over the years I was with him he lied about his work, his income, his relationships, his family, his criminal record, his location and his experiences. He told me he worked for the intelligence services as an IT expert. He lied about calling me from a war zone where children were lying dead in the street, showing me photographs of their mangled bodies. He was deceptive, deceitful, underhand, unscrupulous, manipulative and dishonest – about everything.

Just thinking about the volume and pathology of his lying made me angry. Nothing he had told me was true; nothing had been real.

Score: 2

Cunning and manipulative

This is different to pathological lying: being cunning and manipulative is defined as the use of deception to cheat, con or defraud others for personal gain along with a ruthlessness reflected by the lack of concern for the victims.

Why had Will Jordan lied to me so much? Was it really worth the money? He had taken me for just under £200,000 but for someone with the capacity to make £10,000 per month, that doesn't really seem worth the six years he invested in defrauding me. So at first, I couldn't work out what his 'personal gain' would be. Then I realised that the money he took from me was irrelevant; to him it was just a measure of the control he had over me. I am sure that the money came in useful to help set up new victims – the same way I had initially been wined and dined – but ultimately it was never about the cash.

He didn't really need the money he took from me and our children – it was just a game in his eyes. And in his game it didn't matter how much distress or anxiety it caused me or my family.

Score: 2

Lack of remorse or guilt

When Will Jordan found out I had met his other wife in April 2006, he showed no remorse or guilt whatsoever. Even when I challenged him with the discovery that there were no 'unsavouries' threatening to kidnap and murder my children, and knew he'd been manipulating and conning me for years, he didn't show a glimmer of shame. Indeed, Will Jordan spent a long time trying to pull me back into his orbit – he called me regularly asking me to let him come visit and explain, but I never agreed, just letting him talk on the phone. He never apologised nor took responsibility for his actions but continued to say that all was 'not as it seemed' and everything would be explained in time. Even though I had met his legal wife, he still asked me to have faith in him. This time it wasn't working though. His spell over me had been broken. I carried on talking to him over those first few months after I'd ended the relationship to try and gather as much information as I could. Only once did I ever get a sense that Will Jordan had answered me honestly.

One day just a month after I had found out the truth, he called me from the car. He was driving somewhere but sounded quite drunk. He said he was sorry and that I deserved better than he had treated me, but it was not a heartfelt apology, it was flippant and cursory. I asked him again why he had done what he had done to me. He answered, 'Oh Mary, I'm just a bastard, don't you know that now?'

Score: 2

Shallow affect

Shallow affect is a significant reduction in appropriate emotional responses to situations and events. It was with pain that I remembered the births of my children and how he responded to events that should have been the highlight of a father's life. A moment of pure joy and wonder, but in his case both occasions were something just to be missed. All the way through both pregnancies Will Jordan had told me he would be there for the birth, that nothing would keep him away. He said they were 'miracle babies' as he'd thought himself infertile all his adult life. When I went into labour I texted him and got numerous excited replies saying he was on his way, that he was nearby, that he was almost there! As I was giving birth I was also watching the door, expecting my husband to burst in at any moment. But on both occasions he just didn't arrive. For days afterwards he said that he was just about to come home but that circumstances beyond his control (to do with his work in the intelligence services) had kept him away.

Having met his legal wife, we compared dates, and during the time I was in labour he was with her and their children. He had not in any way been stressed or concerned. He had simply been psychologically torturing me for his own entertainment.

Score: 2

Callousness and lack of empathy

Callousness and lack of empathy is described as a lack of feeling toward people in general: being cold, contemptuous, inconsiderate and tactless. Reading through this checklist brought up all sorts of emotions and thoughts for me. Like knocking off a scab you think is almost healed, only to find virulent infection underneath. I think it was the realisation of his total lack of empathy that really hit home the most. One incident comes to mind with a realisation and an anger that still exists today. Will Jordan had told me he was home for a few days and was at his offices in George Street in Edinburgh and asked if I could come and pick him up. So I put three-year-old Robyn in her car seat and baby Eilidh into the baby seat and drove there. I texted him on arrival to say we were there and he immediately responded saying he was just finishing up and would be down in a few minutes. I waited. Ten minutes later I texted again, asking what was taking so long. He again texted back immediately, saying he was now on his way down. I waited. Robyn and I watched the buildings trying to guess which door he would come out of. Ten minutes later I texted again asking where he was, and got a reply that he was coming, sorry he'd been delayed. Robyn and I started to sing songs together. Another ten minutes and I tried to call. I got a text saying that a colleague had stopped him on the stairs and he just had to do something quickly first. Luckily Eilidh was asleep but I was running out of songs to sing with Robyn. I texted again fifteen minutes later, getting rather annoyed and got apologies and that he would tell his colleagues he had to go. Another ten minutes went by and another text. Just silence. Robyn was getting irritable and hungry. She wasn't alone. I tried calling but got no answer and then texted again to say I was leaving. I got another quick reply saying that he had finished and was on his way out the door. Then everything went quiet again and I got no further responses. When I finally left I had been sitting there with two small children for two hours.

I found out when talking to his other wife that Will Jordan had not even been in Edinburgh that day. He had been with her having a nice relaxing family day out. He had just wanted to see how long he could make me wait.

Not only was he callous and lacking in empathy, he was actively and sadistically going out of his way to make my situation worse just for his own amusement.

Score: 2

Parasitic lifestyle

Everything that Will Jordan does is parasitic. He intentionally and callously manipulated me and exploited me financially, taking me for every penny I had and quite a few that I didn't as well. He convinced me that our children were in danger from blackmailers who were going to kidnap them and rip bits off my babies to send through the post if we didn't come up with the money. He encouraged me to sell my flat to raise funds, then my life insurance policy, and then to borrow money from my family as well. Meanwhile he took out credit cards in my name and ran up bills to the tune of £56,000.

Score: 2

Poor behavioural controls

Will Jordan only ever once got angry with me – when I told the police my husband was driving my car. But as I started to talk to other victims, I was told about several occasions when he had 'lost it'. Alice Kean was defrauded of £4,500 by Will Jordan, the man she had thought was her fiancé in 2005. She initially set up a police sting to catch him red-handed when he used her credit card to pay for his car repairs and this set the ball rolling with regards to his capture and exposure. Alice told me of a time when he drove all the way from London to her home – a journey of several hours – pounding the steering wheel in fury and refusing to speak to her, even though they had not had any cross words. Another victim told me how Will Jordan had flown off the handle and slammed her against a wall, gripping her by the throat as he yelled in her face.

Score: 2

Sexual promiscuity

The very fact that his wife and nanny were both impregnated by him when he started sleeping with me is evidence that he was sexually promiscuous. However, the more I looked into Will Jordan's past, the more victims I found. As a snapshot, I found that in 2005 he had two wives and five fiancées, but throughout the years he was in the UK there were many women who had borne him children and women who had terminated pregnancies by him, most of their relationships overlapping with each other. After finding out the truth, I phoned up numbers I didn't recognise from his phone bill and checked out items from credit cards to find flowers that were sent to women that none of the known victims ever received, and hotels that when interviewed told me he'd stayed in a double room with a woman resembling none of the victims I knew. So the women I actually know about are likely to be the tip of a very screwed-up iceberg: I have no idea how he managed to keep it up.

Score: 2

Early behaviour problems

I managed to track down Will Jordan's eldest child (that I know of), whom I called George in *The Bigamist*. George introduced me to his mother, who had been Will Jordan's childhood sweetheart and knew his family background very well. She told me that even as a pre-teen he had been accused of the sexual assault of a girl younger than himself.

Score: 2

Lack of realistic long-term goals

This is characterised by an inability or persistent failure to develop and execute long-term plans and goals, resulting in a nomadic, aimless existence and a lack of direction in life.

I thought about what Will Jordan was trying to achieve in his life – the women and businesses that he was manipulating and stealing money from, the constant lies and games he was playing with people's lives. It was all living in the moment and nothing was being put in place for a future with anyone – not even his children. Instead, he flits from one woman to another, one family to the next, fathering children and aimlessly playing a game whose rules only he knows – if indeed there are any rules at all. Will Jordan used to tell me about our future. He used to entice me with the constant promise that things were just about to get better. He used our future together like a carrot to encourage me forward, but like everything else all his plans were just lies and nothing ever came to fruition. It must have been obvious that he would be caught out one day but he didn't seem to have any contingency plan in place. It was all just about living in the moment and by the seat of his pants – I suppose that was more stimulating for him.

Score: 2

Impulsivity

I had to look up what impulsivity meant, and read that it is the occurrence of behaviours that are unpremeditated and lack reflection or planning; a lack of deliberation; acting without considering the consequences; an inability to resist temptation, frustrations or urges; foolhardy, rash, unpredictable, erratic and reckless behaviour.

Everything Will Jordan does appears to be calculated but there is an element of impulsivity to his actions, such as when he decides to 'up' the game. There is no thought of the consequences to his actions.

One specific incident came to mind of when Will Jordan finally met my sister, who was back on a visit from Japan. When I first met him, Will told me that he had lived and worked in Japan for a couple of years and spoke fluent Japanese, even though he knew that my eldest sister, Lisa, lived in Japan and was married to a Japanese man. Every time my sister was home, Will Jordan was called away to work at the last minute. Until one day when they finally met in September 2002 after Will Jordan and I had been together for nearly two years.

Lisa was the most suspicious of all my family, having not yet met him and having wondered if Will Jordan was a Walter Mitty-type character. She decided she would test out his language skills in Japanese by asking him a simple question that would require more than a 'yes' or 'no' answer. Lisa and her husband were staying with my mother whilst they were in Scotland and so we went to visit for lunch. We arrived and all settled around my mother's kitchen dining table with six-month-old baby Eilidh in a high chair. Everyone was getting along very well and then my sister asked her question out of the blue, in Japanese.

She never got an answer and at the time didn't even notice.

The extremely well-designed and stable high chair that Eilidh was sitting in fell over backwards! With my baby's terrified screams the conversation was immediately forgotten in favour of frantically rushing around to pick her up and check she was all right. The aftermath of checking her head for bumps and calming down a screaming baby went on for some time and unsurprisingly Will Jordan was called away to work shortly after.

At the time I thought that Eilidh must have managed to push herself away from the dining table. It didn't occur to any of us in the slightest that Will Jordan had kicked over his own baby's high chair simply to avoid answering a question and admitting he couldn't say more than a phrase or two in Japanese.

Score: 2

Irresponsibility

Will Jordan had no sense of duty or loyalty to family or friends and engaged in behaviour that put others at risk. He made no attempt to manage his finances and his work was either non-existent, careless or sloppy. Irresponsibility is defined as a repeated failure to fulfil or honour obligations and commitments such as not paying bills, defaulting on loans, performing slapdash work, being absent or late for jobs, or failing to honour contractual agreements. There are so many incidences of Will Jordan being irresponsible that it is hard to pin down any one example. He was always late for work, he never paid bills, his work for a large software company and a cinema complex was slipshod at best (if undertaken at all). He failed to honour contractual agreements of any type – including a marriage contract.

As for loans, he had borrowed money from almost all of his victims right back to Devi and never paid any of it back. It's actually very hard to think of any area where he *wasn't* irresponsible!

Score: 2

Failure to accept responsibility for own actions

Will Jordan always finds excuses for his behaviour – including making up missions, disasters, deaths and illnesses to explain his actions.

One example springs immediately to mind. The man I spoke to called Malcolm was paying Will Jordan to code his websites and got frustrated with the work not being done. Will Jordan gave Malcolm excuse after excuse as to why the work wasn't finished all the while invoicing him for more and more work. When the excuses started to run thin Will Jordan admitted to Malcolm that his wife had cancer and was not handling the condition very well. She had had a nervous breakdown and 'lost her mind', as he put it. As such, it was making his life very difficult, taking up his time and attention but that he was trying his best to balance that and his work. Malcolm was touched at his dedication to his wife and finally understood the reason for all the delays. Will Jordan said that she needed an operation in London but that he didn't have the money to stay there; Malcolm lent him the funds to rent an apartment for a week in Knightsbridge. Much to Malcolm's horror, the bill came in for the rent and Will Jordan had used it for two weeks (to have Devi and the then sixteen-year-old George come over to London for a visit from the USA). Malcolm tried everything to get the work out of Will Jordan, even tracking him down to his home in Lancashire and waiting in a hotel for Jordan to arrive and hand over the work already 'done'. Although Will Jordan promised hour by hour that he was coming, he was on his way, he had just caught the train, he was getting a taxi, he never turned up. Instead his wife arrived at Malcolm's hotel room at 7 a.m. the next morning, demanding to talk to Malcolm and saying that she knew he was Will Jordan's MI6 handler. Mrs Jordan was frantic and disorientated. Malcolm believed that she was very confused and felt sorry for her, especially as he thought she was dying of cancer. It made Malcolm more sympathetic to Will Jordan as he could see he had a lot on his plate with a sick and deranged wife.

Malcolm reassured Mrs Jordan that he was not who she thought he was, and she left, only to return ten minutes later and demand that he come outside with her. He walked around the parking lot with her as she stated that she *knew* he was Will Jordan's MI6 handler and that his real name was 'Michael'. She demanded that he talk to her about what was going on. Malcolm again just tried to stay calm and treat her with kid gloves. Finally she left.

Will Jordan didn't reply to any more of Malcolm's messages and never showed up. Malcolm went away the next day, empty-handed, but with a deeper sympathy for everything Will Jordan was going through. All the time this was going on, Will Jordan was with me on honeymoon at Shieldhill Castle.

Score: 2

Many short-term marital relationships

This was a 'doh' moment. Will Jordan is a bigamist and I had already discovered at least one other marriage: to Alexis when he was twenty-three years old. He had at least two wives in 2005, as well as having been engaged to three other women at the same time. At this point, the PCL-R seemed like a personality profile specifically designed to describe Will Jordan himself.

Score: 2

Juvenile delinquency

Devi told me many stories about Will Jordan's past. Having been his first girlfriend she knew about his misbehaviour as a child, including sexual assault, cheque fraud and going on the run to Canada by the age of eighteen. Juvenile delinquency is defined as behavioural problems between the ages of thirteen and eighteen years old that are mostly crimes or clearly involve aspects of antagonism, exploitation, aggression, manipulation or a callous, ruthless tough-mindedness.

Devi told me how she had allowed Will Jordan to use her bank card to take out $20 to $30 for food, but instead he had posted a deposit envelope stating a credit of $200 and immediately taken that out in cash on her card, putting her account into overdraft. He had flouted his parents' rules and regulations by hiding Devi in their basement when she was kicked out of her family home and taken her on the run to Canada when he was released from prison for cheque fraud. Devi never found out what he was actually on the run from but told me that once in Canada Will Jordan had immediately started to con people. She also told me that he had been jailed for impersonating a police officer as well as for carrying throwing stars (a particularly aggressive weapon). Devi discovered she was pregnant and went home to New Jersey, where she didn't see Will Jordan for another five years. All of this happened before 1983, when Will Jordan turned eighteen years old.

Score: 2

Revocation of conditional release

One of the crimes Will Jordan was charged with in 2006 was not registering his address under the Sexual Offences Act. One of the hardest parts of this whole situation was coming to terms with the fact that Will Jordan was a convicted paedophile. He had pleaded guilty in 1997 to sexual offences against a girl under the age of thirteen and was given a fifteen-month sentence. He was released after seven months on good behaviour. (In the UK, offenders automatically serve half the time given and spend the rest 'on licence', bound to certain conditions or they go back to prison for the rest of the time.) On top of that, his condition of release was to register his address with the authorities as a sex offender for ten years. So the charges of not registering his address was literally a revocation of conditional release.

Score: 2

Criminal versatility

Criminal versatility is defined as a diversity of type of criminal offence, regardless of whether the person has been arrested or convicted for them. Looking at the history of what I know, Will Jordan has been convicted of cheque fraud (USA), fraud (USA), and sexual assault of a girl under the age of thirteen (UK). I have also been told he was convicted of impersonating a government official (Canada), and possessing banned weapons (possessing throwing stars in Canada). With the more recent additions in 2006 of bigamy, fraud, firearms (taser) and not registering his address under the Sexual Offences Act in the UK, Will Jordan is the very definition of 'criminally versatile'.

Score: 2

Total

By my amateur calculation of the Psychopath Checklist (Revised), and from what I intimately know of my ex's actions, Will Jordan easily scores 40 points out of an available 40 points.

By now, there was no doubt in my mind that he is a psychopath. Suddenly things started to make sense and why he did what he did to me came into sharp focus.

Knowing that Will Jordan is a psychopath changed everything for me. It was clear that his behaviour had nothing to do with me and there was nothing I had done to deserve the treatment he had inflicted. There was no amount of love I could have given him that would have 'cured' him, no amount of nurturing or support that would have made him a better man or father. I had promised to love him 'in sickness and in health' and had felt that I had broken that promise by leaving the relationship. But in truth he was not 'sick', it was just that the person he had pretended to be didn't exist. I was freed from my bonds of matrimony and the promises that I had earnestly made in good faith. It meant I did not have to feel guilty for giving up on the relationship.

Now I knew what he was: a predator, an unemotional machine programmed for complete self-gratification with literally no empathy for any of his victims, including his children. He did not have the capacity to love, nor did he feel the remotest twinge of guilt for what he had done. Nothing of the man I used to love remained. I could now see that the man he had pretended to be was a fiction, invented to manipulate me into loving him. With that knowledge, my love for him evaporated like a dream, leaving only the realisation of the monster he truly was.

Shattering the Silence

Knowing Will Jordan is a psychopath helped me feel grounded again. It gave me something to focus on and the language to both explain what had happened as well as to research further. I became fascinated and started to read everything I could about psychopaths, sociopaths and narcissists. I devoured articles online and books written by experts and victims alike.

I thought long and hard about how to talk to the children about Will Jordan being a psychopath. I had already made the decision that they had been lied to enough and that I would never lie to them ever about anything. No matter what, I would be honest with them and honest with the world. Lies poison lives and I would have no part of them.

I had already told them that their dad had another family and that he was in prison on remand, awaiting trial. I had explained that when they did something bad, I made them sit on their beds and think about it, but a grown-up is supposed to already know right from wrong. When a grown-up breaks the law they are sent to court where a judge decides if they have done wrong, and how long to send the adult to jail for – to think about what they have done.

I was concerned that the children would blame themselves for Will Jordan's absence and grow up thinking it was something to do with them that he was not home and being a loving father to them. I felt it was important that they grew up understanding the whole truth and that it was absolutely not their fault. Zach was still only a year old and too young to understand, so I left him having a nap and sat Robyn and Eilidh down to talk to them. I explained that Will Jordan had a personality disorder which meant that he didn't have empathy, that he simply wasn't able to feel guilt or regret, nor feel love for anybody at all. I said that if their father had been blind, they wouldn't blame themselves that he couldn't see them – a simple concept they could easily understand. I added that Will Jordan was incapable of love, even for his own children, so they shouldn't blame themselves for the fact that he didn't love them. He simply didn't have the ability to do so.

Robyn and Eilidh seemed to understand and asked lots of questions, ones I was now able to answer in simple and uncomplicated terms. It was a remarkably unemotional conversation and one that was repeated whenever they asked something else.

My children have grown up confident that I will always tell them the truth, no matter what. They know that I respect them enough to do that. Sometimes that has meant having to answer awkward questions or being embarrassed, but there is a freedom in always telling the truth and there is nothing my children don't know about me. There is nothing I have to fear 'coming to light' in the future.

Getting the publishing deal helped me enormously, not just because it meant I would have a focus for writing it all down but it also gave me something to work towards and deadlines to achieve. It offered a future career and a chance to earn back some money, something I was desperately short of as I was still in incredible debt with the £56,000 owing on my credit cards.

It felt like an insurmountable sum and the debt collectors had been calling since April 2006. They were relentless. Every day I would get calls from various people asking for payment. Each time I would explain that I had been conned and had nothing to give. I was on incapacity benefits by now and barely making ends meet. In Scotland, you cannot declare bankruptcy – one of your creditors has to take you to court and *make* you bankrupt. I would ask them to take me to court so the nightmare round of daily calls would stop, but they could see there was no point wasting more of their money on a court case so would just tell me they would call again tomorrow.

It was soul-destroying. Every phone call opened wounds and rubbed in the salt. It was a catch-22 situation that seemed impossible to escape. Day after day I had to answer the calls. There seemed no end to it.

Before she died, my mother had found out about the Protected Trust Deed situation in Scotland where you put all your assets in a fund and then offer a small percentage of the debt (such as 15p for each £1) to the creditors straight away. Alternatively they can accept getting the full amount of the debt repaid monthly but in the form of pennies each month for the next fifty years. The Deed seemed like the only option I had to dig myself out of the financial hole I was in. However, I would need some capital to put into the fund to make it attractive enough for my creditors to accept.

Selling my story to the *Daily Mail* in November 2006 was not a highpoint of my life but due to the media interest around the trial I felt it would give me a chance to put some money towards the Protected Trust Deed. A friend who was a television presenter for Sky News put me in touch with a trustworthy independent journalist called Marcello Mega and we arranged to meet at the café in the Chamber Street Museum in Edinburgh. I didn't even give him my name at first because I was so nervous about him just running with the story without my permission. However, Cello turned out to be brilliant. He was sympathetic to my situation and we worked on the outline story together. He also knew who to talk to and managed to negotiate a good deal for me with the newspaper.

The article was pretty good except that the editor added a final comment at the end which rather missed the whole point of coercive control and gaslighting. He wrote, 'If ever there was a story to prove the age-old adage that love is blind, this is surely it.' The paper also insisted that I wore a dress for the photo shoot which simply is not me! They actually brought the dress with them and told me to wear it. I didn't refuse because they were paying me but it felt like I was selling a part of myself that I wasn't particularly comfortable with.

When the *Daily Mail* article came out, I experienced my first online trolling attacks. People commented under the online article about how 'desperate' I must have been and how 'unattractive' and 'needy' I was. More than anything, the comments noted how 'stupid' I must have been to have fallen for Will Jordan's lies and believed that he loved me, that it should have been obvious he was conning me from the very start. It is extraordinary how cruel people can be when they can hide behind an anonymous computer keyboard.

It hurt. I felt judged and humiliated. I had been the victim of a crime and a systematic abuse of my psychological, emotional and financial state. I questioned whether I should have gone public and the feelings of insecurity and uncertainty threatened to sweep over me again. It felt like I was being victimised all over again. I wondered whether I shouldn't have spoken out, should maybe have stayed silent. That word again. Silent. Voiceless, hidden, small, insignificant, nothing. The first rule of any abuser is to keep their victim silent. Ensure they are isolated and alone, that they don't speak out or articulate (and thereby make sense of) what is happening to them.

Then I had a revelation. If my children in later life came to me with a problem like this – if they said they had been bullied, or people had said nasty things about them – would I have told them to stay silent, to hide away and hang their heads in shame? Certainly not! I wanted my children to know they should never feel ashamed of being a victim of a crime and to do that I needed to show them by example.

So I pulled myself up with a snap. The trolls were providing another type of abuse, and I was not going to be kept silent any more.

I realised that 'victim shaming' is a form of self-preservation. If these people can blame the victim then they themselves are safe. Because *they* won't be as foolish, or gullible, unattractive or just plain unlucky. I realised that just like in the past when rape victims were ostracised, it would take someone standing up and talking about it to change societal views. Someone had to stand up and be counted, open up the conversation and show that it is *never* the victim's fault. No one should *ever* feel ashamed of having been a victim of a crime. One of those 'someones' was going to be me.

The trolls actually fuelled my commitment to talk publicly about the subject and help other victims know they can speak up too.

Having been signed off on incapacity benefits I had an income of about £90 per week but received government help with the rent as well. So I had time to gather myself and recover. It was not a glamorous existence but I managed to make ends meet and was already very good at surviving on a budget towards the end of my relationship with Will Jordan.

Once my car was taken away I started cycling everywhere. I had a child seat on the front of my bicycle where my one-year-old son Zach would sit, and a tag-along joined at the back for four-year-old Eilidh. My seven-year-old daughter Robyn would cycle beside me. We all had fun cycle helmets as well – mine had a cover with dragon spikes and a tail hanging down. All in all, we looked like a travelling circus when we went out. People used to smile and wave to us, which the children loved.

At the time I didn't know what the future held but did know that whatever job I finally ended up doing, my priority was to be available for the children. They only had one parent left and I couldn't be working all hours to pay for the vicious cycle of childcare so I could work. With one daughter already at primary school and another about to start, I would have to think of a job I could do that would allow me to be there for them – to drop them off and pick them up from school, as well as be around for the holidays. It was not an easy problem to solve and I realised pretty quickly that the only real option was self-employment. But doing what?

I didn't want to go back to being a business adviser or marketing consultant – I didn't feel I could face telling people what they should do, especially having gone public with my own bad judgement at having been taken in by a con man. I had loved certain aspects of that job, particularly the training courses I ran and the workshops I held, but certainly didn't feel ready to go back to providing business training.

In November 2006 I got £5,000 for the *Daily Mail* article, a lump sum to put into the Protected Trust Deed; it was a start at least. By the end of 2006 I managed to raise a total of around £8,000 and all the creditors on the Protected Trust Deed accepted the terms. It was galling to come up with even more money to pay off what were essentially Will Jordan's debts, but at least that was the end of it and I was finally debt-free.

CONVICTION

My bigamist husband was convicted on 22 November 2006 and twenty-eight days later, on 21 December, he was sentenced to five years in prison for bigamy, fraud, possessing a firearm and not registering his address under the Sexual Offences Act. I felt like I had been holding my breath during the trial and sentencing and exhaled a sigh of relief when the judge handed down the sentence. It meant so much to me that the courts had acknowledged what he had done as a crime. And Judge Thomas Corrie's statement was even more significant to my recovery, because it spelled out what Will Jordan had done in no uncertain terms.

> 'Mr Jordan, you are forty-one, a con man, a convicted pae-dophile, a bigamist and an inveterate exploiter of vulner-able women. You have little or no regard for their feelings despite a belated expression of remorse. You have caused significant emotional damage to three women and finan-cial loss to certainly one – Alice Kean.

> 'I have read the victim impact statements of Alice Kean and your bigamist wife Mary Turner Thomson, who is present in the court. You are to be sentenced regarding the deception of Alice Kean for wrongful use of her credit card and also two separate charges of not registering your

address. It is clear that you pay little regard for that legal nicety.

'In addition, a taser was found in the car, a car that you couldn't afford without cheating others.

'You pleaded not guilty on 7 July 2006 on counts 1 to 5, all deception offences, but guilty of bigamy. You also pleaded guilty to possession of a prohibited weapon and to one of two counts of not registering your address under the Sexual Offences Act.

'The position put shortly is that you obtained the trust and love of Alice Kean, and took £4,500 off her by deception by making various false assurances regarding paying her back and that you wanted to marry her. You abused her credit card, which is counts 2 to 5. The stun gun deserves no further comment. Sex-offender offences show that you do not care about keeping the authorities informed. I do not accept that you did not know the length of time you had to register for.

'I make it clear that I have read and taken into account all the papers, prosecution and victim impact statements which demonstrate women emotionally broken. The path to recovery for both women will be a difficult one.

'Regarding the pre-sentence report stating the likelihood of re-offending as being "low to medium", I simply do not agree with it. Looking at the facility of dishonesty, I find it hard to believe that the risk of re-offending is . . . "low".'

The judge then addressed the court regarding sentencing.

'For the counts of fraud I give twenty-one months. For the bigamy none of the previous cases were of particular assistance apart from immediate custodial sentence. This bigamy is a serious one and the effect is substantial, requiring being properly sentenced. Therefore I award it twenty-one months, making forty-two months so far.

'For the taser, the sentence is nine months, making fifty-one months' running total. For the two counts of not registering his address, I think that it is of the utmost importance and of great public concern that the authorities are kept informed. I therefore give three months and six months making nine months consecutive, bringing the total sentence to sixty months, or five years. Credit will be awarded for the 105 days already served on remand.'

The Crown Prosecutor was delighted with the outcome as he was not certain whether Will Jordan would even get prison time at all. It depended on the judge understanding the extent of what he had done. Will Jordan's defence for bigamy was that he had married me because I was pregnant and he didn't know what else to do. His defence for fraud was that Alice had given him all the money but found out that he was married and decided to extract revenge by getting him arrested. His ploy for getting around not registering as a sex offender was going to be that it was a mistake and he didn't think he had to register any more. And the excuse for the taser was that he was American and knew guns were banned in the UK but didn't realise tasers were a problem. He wanted to break down the charges into smaller chunks to make what he had done seem more reasonable – he would have looked like a fool and a cad, but he would have beaten the system. It was my victim impact statement that changed everything.

I stood up and insisted on having that statement submitted and this showed the judge how all Will Jordan's crimes tied together, how everything was part of his psychopathic game of manipulation.

Knowing that he was going to be behind bars for a few years was reassuring. I had almost finished writing the second draft of the book and was determined not to serve as a victim to him (or anyone) any more. I wanted to stand up to him as well as stand up for myself – and here was a judge standing up with me and it felt massively validating.

As I left the sentencing a woman called Helen approached me. She was another victim of Will Jordan but hadn't seen him since she had been eight months pregnant with his child. She'd had his parents' telephone number and phoned them to report on his behaviour, but they had just fobbed her off and seemed to show no interest in their future grandchild. When she confronted Will Jordan about his lies he had shrugged and walked away, never to be seen again until the day he was sentenced. Helen had seen the story in the *Daily Mail* and decided to come along and witness the trial for herself. Another kindred spirit had found me.

When I had met William Allen Jordan in the year 2000, the Internet was just starting up and there was no information about him online. There was no capability at the time to search images and the basic search engines assumed that 'Will' was a question rather than a name. As a result, a search on 'Will Jordan' resulted in statements about a sportsman called Jordan, or the Middle Eastern nation. Although I had tried to do my due diligence and research him a little when we first met, there was nothing available about him. I was determined that when the next victim started to research who he was, they would have all the information available for them to make a good judgement.

New Year, New Start

Four days after sentencing we celebrated Christmas for the first time without Mum. It broke my heart to be without her but I tried to make it as cheerful for the children as I could. We spent time with my father who was coping as best he knew how and as usual caught up with my siblings and niblings.

At last, 2006 was coming to an end. So much had happened that year and it was good to see the back of it. Will Jordan was finally convicted and in jail and my financial troubles were being ironed out.

All year I had talked to various lawyers to ask what I should do about my bigamous marriage and how to extricate myself from it. One suggested I would need to get a divorce, which would be costly. Another suggested that I could get it annulled but was not sure how I would go about doing that. No one could give a definitive answer and most advised waiting until the trial was over. (To be fair, there had only been ten cases of bigamy in the UK the year before so it demanded rather specialist legal knowledge.)

I wanted nothing to do with Will Jordan any more and certainly didn't want to be called 'Mrs Jordan', nor did I want my children to be reminded of the connection with him every time their name was called in class. So I got in touch with the Registry Office on 31 December and told them I wanted to change my children's names.

At first the woman at the Registry Office was cagey. She asked if I was married as my husband would have rights over the children's names as well. I briefly explained that I had got married but that he had just been convicted of bigamy. That I had no idea how I was supposed to extricate myself from the marriage, but that he certainly had lost all rights over the children. The woman was shocked and asked me where he had been convicted and I told her it was Oxford Crown Court. She thanked me and asked if she could call me back later. I was rather surprised but agreed.

Less than five minutes later she called me.

'It's sorted,' she said.

'What is?' I asked, rather confused.

'You were never married. You're still single. I called the Court and they've faxed over the conviction for bigamy which is now attached to your original marriage certificate. Legally, you have never been married. Therefore you don't have to get his permission to change the children's names.'

'Really?' I asked, stunned, as I reflected on the number of meetings and phone calls I'd made trying to sort this out. 'It's that simple?'

The woman went on to explain that the law about altering names was due to change on 1 January 2007 and that you would no longer have to live under a new name for two years before being able to change it legally. That meant we could all change our names immediately, and that Zach – who was only nineteen months old – would be the youngest person to change his name in Scotland at that time.

I was delighted, and she gave us the first appointment for when they opened up after Hogmanay on 2 January 2007. And, just like that, the name Jordan was eradicated from our family.

FIGHTING SPIRIT

Will Jordan was going to be in jail for at least two and a half years but one day he would be out again. I didn't know if he might be angry and seek retribution for my talking to the press, let alone writing a book about him. I was nervous but also refused to live in fear any more. I had a recurring nightmare about him turning up at my door and wanted to know what to do if that ever happened. I decided I needed to learn to defend myself physically and so when one of my best friends, Carina, mentioned she was thinking of joining a local taekwondo martial arts class, I jumped at the chance to do it with her. Taekwondo literally translates as 'the art of fist and foot' and as the legs are generally stronger and longer than arms, using them is more effective in fights, especially when a woman is defending herself against a man. Taekwondo teaches you to use both arms and legs which benefits the fighter in close combat as well as keeping an assailant at a distance.

When we first started classes, I watched people doing the press-ups and physical patterns with ease and wondered how I would ever be able to get to that level. Having been a dancer and gymnast at school and college I was still very flexible but had very little physical strength. The taekwondo patterns helped focus the muscles on moving the right way and my dancer training from my youth helped me learn them step by step. I used to joke that it was taking me so long to get my black belt that I would be a grey belt!

However, my plan was to be a black belt by the time Will Jordan was released from prison, so I trained hard and was very focused. Each time I punched or kicked a pad I pictured his face and it helped me hit that much harder. Not because I wanted to hit him but just that it reminded me that I needed the skill to defend myself.

My children came with me to taekwondo. I didn't have a babysitter nor could I afford one at the time. My two-year-old son used to sit in the corner of the hall and watch as I trained. When he was bored he would try to join in and often held on to my ankles whilst I tried to practise the patterns. My club were extremely supportive and understanding – I had told them about my circumstances, which helped!

I found the training helped build my physical confidence and made me feel more in control. I grew fitter and stronger and started to do press-ups. At first I could only lower myself an inch, then it was a couple of inches, but gradually my strength increased and I was able to keep up with the rest of the class.

My teacher, Paul, has become a great friend and I loved sparring with him. He would dodge and weave, easily blocking any attack I made. It was frustrating but inspiring too. In those early days he would cheekily put his hands down and not guard himself, daring me to try and lay a glove on him. As I got better his guard came up and finally I felt my skill growing, even though I could still never hit him.

The club became more than just somewhere to learn how to defend myself – it became a family and a group of friends whom I truly value. What's more, my children grew up with the club and were adopted into it, joining in as they grew up.

Whilst I was learning to fight I was also working with an editor on the final draft of the book. She was brilliant and asked all the right questions, prompting me to explain in more detail each step of the process and what I went through. Those questions really helped focus my mind and get the last shards of splintered information out of my head.

Then all of a sudden a final draft was finished, a cover designed and agreed, and a launch date fixed. By the summer of 2007 I would be a published author!

DAYTIME TV

My first book was published in 2007. Finally I held a copy in my hand.

It is extraordinary seeing your name on the cover of a book and I felt taller and stronger because of it. I felt awestruck being able to describe myself as an 'author' and was filled with an immense sense of pride. I knew my mother would have been so proud of me as well.

I was sent to London by the publishers to speak on TV and radio to promote the book. I had worked for the BBC for two years from 1987 to 1989 – including working on *EastEnders* and *All Creatures Great and Small* – so I was familiar with television studios. However, being behind the camera was very different to being on it! I have never been keen on being filmed and was initially nervous but it was all part and parcel of being an author and I had to get used to it. It was strange to be talking about myself in that way, but the more I did the easier it was. I found talking about psychopaths fascinating and tried to frame my story around that so victims of other psychopaths could relate to it.

There were about twenty radio shows that wanted to interview me as well as a few TV companies. I had never watched daytime TV so had no idea really of what to expect. The first TV show I did was *This Morning* with Phil Schofield and Fern Britton. I was picked up by car and welcomed on arrival. It was fun to be treated like a VIP, having my hair and make-up professionally done. I was shown to a delightful Green Room where I met the other interviewees – one of the Cheeky

Girls (a Romanian singing duo) who was dating a politician, a boy who had been recovering from anorexia, and Simon Cowell's girlfriend.

Finally I was taken through to the studio and met Phil and Fern during the commercial break. I had worked with Phil Schofield in 1987 at the tail end of his broom cupboard days at Children's BBC and commented on this to Phil before we went on air. He very sweetly said he remembered me. It was a nice connection which made me feel more comfortable on live television for the first time. The interview went well and Phil was suitably shocked by my story. All in all it was a good experience.

Shortly afterwards, in August 2007, I was interviewed by another daytime TV host, and it was all very different. I had to get a taxi to the studio and when I arrived they searched me for weapons! I knew something wasn't right when I had to go through a metal detector to get to the dressing rooms.

There I was, in another TV studio, on a relatively new daytime TV show which I had never heard of before. There was another hair and make-up artist making me presentable, but this time I was put in a private dressing room down a long corridor. At one point I left the dressing room to find a bathroom and was met in the corridor by a man who seemed to be standing guard. He very pointedly asked me where I was going.

'To the loo,' I replied.

'Just stay here. I'll need to check if they're being cleaned,' he said rather gruffly.

That's when I realised they were keeping the interviewees apart. It didn't bode well.

Whilst the guard was away 'checking' if the toilet was being cleaned, the lady in the next dressing room came out and we decided to sit together and chatted. The 'special' programme was supposed to be about victims of con men so we knew we had something in common.

This lady – Renata – had been a victim of the infamous MI5 con man Robert Hendy-Freegard. This was a story I was all too familiar with because *Deceived*, a memoir by another of his victims, Sarah Smith, was one of the many books I'd read on the subject.

◆ ◆ ◆

Robert Hendy-Freegard had convinced three students that he was an MI5 operative and that all three (two girls and a boy) had become the target of an IRA assassination plot.

He was working as a barman in 1992 when he met the three students – Sarah Smith, Maria Hendy and John Atkinson. A fourth student, and friend of theirs, had just committed suicide with a shotgun and Hendy-Freegard overheard them talking about it, which set his plan in action. Hendy-Freegard told the students that he was a Special Branch police officer who was working in the bar undercover to catch members of an IRA cell that was operating there. He convinced all three students that their friend had not committed suicide but had actually been murdered due to having witnessed something the IRA were doing. What's more, MI5 and Special Branch had uncovered a plot to murder all three of them too.

Robert Hendy-Freegard took them all into 'safe house' protection under his control and submitted them to bizarre abuses including having to prove their loyalty in various brutal ways. He persuaded them to cut ties with family and friends to alienate them, and then got them to elicit money from their families as well. He managed to convince John and his parents to give him £300,000 whilst John was put into 'training'.

Maria stayed with him for eight years, giving birth to two of his daughters and living in dire poverty whilst he swanned around in expensive cars and designer suits. After some time John left, and then Maria, but with no contact with the outside world the last victim, Sarah

Smith, remained under his control for ten years, hiding in attics and basements, living in fear and believing that he was her only chance of survival. He would leave her for days at a time, once locked in a bathroom with no food.

He duped a woman called Lesley Gardner in Newcastle and milked her for £16,000 over six years, claiming he had to pay off IRA killers who had been released after the Good Friday Agreement. He also sold her car and kept the money.

Hendy-Freegard met Elizabeth Richardson, a newly married PA working in a Sheffield car dealership, and forced her to change her name and go on the run with him. She spent seventeen months spending nights on park benches and surviving on slices of Mars Bars and water from public toilets. He also persuaded her to take out loans of £6,500 and £8,000 which he pocketed. Eventually Elizabeth was discovered by the police in a hovel in Leicestershire, emaciated and covered in sores.

Hendy-Freegard also targeted Renata when she was buying a car at the same dealership. Renata was heavily pregnant when they met and had recently split from her partner. After selling her a car and striking up a relationship, Hendy-Freegard told her he was spying on someone at the car dealership and eventually convinced her to take out a £15,000 loan for him. Renata also helped house Sarah Smith, who was supposedly in a witness protection program. Hendy-Freegard told Renata that the woman only spoke Spanish so that they wouldn't speak to each other.

Meanwhile Hendy-Freegard was having multiple other relationships. He seduced a high-flying lawyer called Caroline Cowper from whom he stole £14,000: they became engaged, but her family intervened. And in 2002 he became involved in a relationship with an American child psychologist called Kimberley Adams, at which time he 'admitted' to her that he had infiltrated a criminal network and killed a criminal who had threatened to expose him. He even asked Kimberly to marry him but said there was a condition: she would also need to become an agent and cut off all contact with her family. It was her family who called in the FBI, something which eventually led to Hendy-Freegard's arrest.

Kimberly's mother promised to give him the £10,000 he had asked for but would only hand it over in person, saying she would fly to the UK to ensure her daughter was safe and well. When Hendy-Freegard arrived at Heathrow Airport to meet Kimberly's mother and pick up the money, the police arrested him. He claimed innocence and proclaimed it was all part of a conspiracy right up to his trial.

In June 2005 he was convicted of two counts of kidnapping, ten of theft and eight of deception. In September 2005 he was sentenced to life in prison. However, he appealed his kidnapping conviction and astoundingly won his appeal in April 2007 – just four months before I met Renata in the studio – reducing his life sentence to just nine years. To my astonishment, the judge said that his victims were not physically restrained and it was therefore not 'kidnapping'.

◆ ◆ ◆

I had known Sarah Smith's story having read her book, but had been unaware of the large number of other victims Robert Hendy Freegard had targeted. Clearly, here was another psychopathic predator. I told Renata what I had learnt about psychopaths. She was intrigued and said she would do further research herself.

When the daytime TV official came back from checking the bathroom, Renata and I were already deep in conversation and he grudgingly allowed us to share a dressing room. We had a very interesting chat before she was taken through to the studio. It was truly fascinating to talk to another victim of an intricate psychopathic plot.

I finally went out to the studio and sat in a curved armchair in front of a live studio audience. The host, a man called Jeremy Kyle, sat beside me and started to ask me questions. How had I met Will Jordan?

What had happened? The other wife had also agreed to be interviewed and was in the studio but didn't want to be on camera, so they kept her in a back room with her silhouetted outline on a screen and (for some inexplicable reason) her voice that of a Dalek.

At first the interview went smoothly, but gradually Jeremy Kyle's attitude and demeanour started to grate on me. Every time I started to explain about psychopaths he would touch his earpiece and shout, 'I can't hear Lucy! I can't hear Lucy!'

Having worked in TV and video production, I knew this was a deliberate ploy to cut me off so he'd be able to edit around what I was saying. He also moved around the stage, standing up and then sitting on the steps below me when he was talking to the silhouetted outline of Will Jordan's other wife. It was a bizarre way to conduct a television interview and came across as arrogant and unsympathetic.

His attitude towards the other wife was condescending and aggressive, asking her why she had allowed her husband to have affairs and hadn't left him.

I was still talking calmly but was getting irritated with his attitude. He was constantly trying to make me look like an idiot and at one point asked, 'So he told you he was infertile?'

'Yes,' I replied.

'But you got pregnant?'

'Yes,' I replied again simply.

'But you thought he was infertile?'

'Clearly not after I got pregnant!' I said calmly.

He tried asking that question again a couple of times but I kept giving him the same response. This is an interviewing technique to try and elicit the response the interviewer wants. If people keep asking the same question, we try to accommodate them by varying the answer because to keep repeating the same answer makes us feel like a school-child who has got the answer wrong the first time. But I was not going to be intimidated by this interviewer.

Mostly I was furious about the way he was treating the other wife, and by the time the interview was over I was aghast that my publishers had suggested my appearing on this particular programme.

As I left the studio the assistant floor manager said gleefully, 'Isn't he marvellous?'

I stopped and looked her straight in the eye and said, 'No!'

It occurred to me that Kyle ran his studio like Will Jordan or Robert Hendy-Freegard had managed their victims. It was manipulation and had I not been aware of what was going on, I think I would have left feeling totally demoralised and crushed by his patronising manner. I wondered what on earth the producers and director were doing to allow him to behave in this way. What's more, I still struggle to understand why the public liked watching the show.

On leaving I called my agent, who was furious with the publishers for having agreed to the interview, and I have never since done a media show, neither radio nor TV, without first checking it out for myself.

I am glad to say that *The Jeremy Kyle Show* is no longer broadcast. Sadly, an interviewee committed suicide in 2019 after filming a section and the broadcaster initially suspended and then decided to cancel the show indefinitely, including the airing of any previous episodes. The show had only started in 2005 so it was understandable that I had not heard of it at the time in August 2007, but it is still a source of embarrassment to me that I went on it at all.

The Wounded

One good thing that came out of the Jeremy Kyle show was that it gave me and the other wife the chance to talk. She had been against the publication of my book whilst I had been writing it, and my publishers told me that she'd been on the phone to them several times, threatening to sue if they went ahead. However, she approached me after the show and suggested we go and have coffee.

We went to the train station and sat at a little round table by a coffee stand. She seemed much less tense than when I had first met her on 5 April 2006: the day we had both discovered we were married to the same man. She was also understandably much more friendly. She told me she had finally read my book and admitted she was now pleased I'd written it. To my relief she said that it had helped her understand both her own and my situation far better than before because it allowed her to see the bigger picture. This came as a huge relief to me. I had never wanted my going public to be a source of distress for any of the other victims. I knew it had to be done but was also acutely aware that some of his victims might still feel emotionally traumatised and would rather no one knew about our separate ordeals at all – which is why I had not used any of their real names.

After that she used to call me regularly. Finally she needed to talk – and talk she did. The phone calls usually lasted about up to an hour and a half each, two to three times a week. She needed to vent and so

I just listened, giving her a sounding board that would hopefully help her recover from sixteen years of abuse.

We compared notes. She told me that Will Jordan had never taken a driving test and never possessed a driving licence either in the USA or in the UK. This shocked me, considering the amount he drove about, and suddenly why he wouldn't hire a car for himself made sense. We discussed dates and times, clarifying some of the things he'd been doing when he had lied about being out of the country.

I discovered why his feet were in such a bad state in 2005 after he said he'd been trapped during a supposed massacre in Jenin (in the Palestinian territories) for three months. The truth was he'd worn boots two sizes too small for him for several weeks before coming home to me. She'd asked him why he was wearing the boots when they clearly hurt him, and he just replied that he liked how they looked. In truth, he was damaging his feet intentionally to have physical evidence of his lies for my benefit.

◆　◆　◆

In researching *The Bigamist*, I learnt a lot from his victims about other incidents of his own self-harming in order to provide proof. One of his victims didn't want to have any more children so she suggested that she would get her tubes tied. Will Jordan insisted that was too invasive and offered to have a vasectomy instead. He duly went off to have the procedure done and came back with what looked like two cigarette burns on the outside of his testicles. Strangely enough, she got pregnant again and he said the procedure must have failed.

I wondered how he could do such painful and distressing things to himself simply to perpetuate a lie, so I looked it up.

Research into psychopaths has shown they have no emotional response to other people but also have no empathic emotional response to themselves either. The researchers had done experiments where they'd strapped volunteers into an electric chair and told them they'd receive an electric shock. Their heart rate immediately quickened. They received the shock and the rate jumped up high then slowly came down again. The researchers would then tell the volunteer that they'd receive another shock and the heart rate jumped right back up to high in anticipation of the pain they'd receive. However, when the researchers conducted the same experiment on a psychopath (as identified through the PCL-R), their heart rate remained stable until they received the shock, when it jumped to high and then back to normal again. When told they'd receive another shock it remained normal until the pain actually hit.

As well as having no empathy for other people, psychopaths have no empathy for their future selves either. It is not that they do not feel the pain, just that they don't care that their future self is going to feel it.

Empathic people empathise with their future selves as if they are another person: we imagine ourselves the next day, week, month or year as though we are thinking of someone we care about.

Knowing that, Will Jordan going to burn himself with a cigarette would not have elicited an emotional response from him. Even a few seconds after feeling the first shock of pain, and knowing he was going to burn himself again, it still would not have elicited any response. He will have felt the pain, but no distress that he was about to feel pain.

My long telephone conversations with the other wife covered an enormous amount of ground and I got to know and understand her much better than I had before. She told me all about the other victims she knew of, including the nannies she had employed to look after their children. I already knew about one of the nannies who had two children by Will Jordan, but the other wife told me about another young girl who had lost her life because of him. This girl, only nineteen years old, I believe, started nannying for the family. In a very short space of time Will Jordan seduced her. When the wife found out, he rejected the girl and she lost her job and her home, having to leave the house in disgrace. The other wife then told me how the girl had turned up again, having taken an overdose of paracetamol. They took her to the hospital but it was too late to save her. Her liver failed and she died slowly and in great pain.

One incident that came to light when we compared notes was extraordinarily revealing. The other wife told me about an incident in October 2002 when Will Jordan had told her his MI6 handler, Michael, was staying in a hotel just near her home. She had been in regular contact with Michael over the years and admitted to being a little in love with him even though they'd never met in person. His being so close by was too tempting for her to resist so she went to the hotel to meet him. When she arrived at the hotel room, Michael answered the door and immediately looked uncomfortable – he refused to speak to her, stating that he was just a businessman who worked with Will Jordan. She left and started to go home, but within five minutes of leaving, got a text from Michael saying that he was being bugged and she needed to understand that he couldn't talk to her. She immediately turned around and went back. Knocking on his door once again she insisted that he accompany her to the parking lot, where they walked around in circles. The other wife tried to get Michael to talk but he insisted that he was just a businessman and refused to discuss anything with her. Again she left confused and angry. Once again she got a text within five minutes from Michael telling her that his phone was bugged, not the room, and that he genuinely couldn't talk to her but they would meet and talk in person soon.

I had already heard this story from the other person's perspective – Malcolm, the businessman Will Jordan had defrauded and whom he had told that his wife was dying from cancer and had lost her mind. Will Jordan had been posing online as his own MI6 handler to his wife, and Malcolm had given him the perfect opportunity to show her that this person was indeed real. However, how did Will Jordan know to text as soon as his wife had left? At the time, Will Jordan was with me on honeymoon at Shieldhill Castle in Scotland, hundreds of miles away. So how was he keeping track of her?

I remembered that I had read about modern bugging devices and asked the wife what kind of phone she had. It was a small blue Nokia phone that Will Jordan had given her. A quick Google search provided the answer. At the time you could buy a bugging device that looked and worked exactly like that Nokia phone – although it had one additional special feature. Will Jordan could dial up the phone he had given his wife and enter an additional number code – her phone would answer without ringing and without showing her it was even on. It was a domestic bugging device. Although we are not 100% sure that this is what he did, it seems to fit the evidence and would explain how he knew what she was doing and who she had been talking to.

I remembered that whilst on honeymoon, Will Jordan had spent some time listening to music whilst I read a book, but now I realised that he had not been listening to music at all; he had been listening in to his wife and his client meeting at the hotel, allowing him to continue manipulating them both in his own twisted game.

The other wife told me many other stories about what he had done to her throughout their marriage which I will not relate here because she does not want her story to be made public. I suspect she still feels embarrassed and ashamed about things he manipulated her into doing. And it makes my story seem like a fairy tale. However, that is not my story to tell.

It seemed like she so desperately wanted to believe that he loved her. She wanted her children to have been loved by him and for her family to have been special to him in some way, which I suppose they were because she had not kicked him out and had given him somewhere to come back to between games. They were his base camp. Her desperation to be special to him was dangerous though, and I felt it kept her vulnerable to him. She always seemed to be in danger of being dragged back to him and I was worried what might happen to her and their children when he was free again.

I tried to keep her grounded and out of his clutches but to accept that he was truly a psychopath meant that sixteen years of her life was a lie. That is not an easy thing to do.

So day by day, and week by week, the phone calls from her came.

◆ ◆ ◆

I was still in touch with the other victims as well and we talked regularly, sharing stories and experiences. New victims also came forwards. One woman had seen the Jeremy Kyle show and allowed me to share her story in the updated version of my book that came out in 2008.

We were all wounded but together we started to heal. Knowing there were other women out there that knew and understood what we had been through was incredibly helpful. As a group we compared dates and got a fairly good idea of where he had been and when. There were definite gaps though and it was clear there had been additional victims who had never come forward. Families, children, businesses and women whom he had violated but who either didn't know the truth or didn't want to be in contact with the rest of us. Through our collective knowledge, we plotted an average of three to five women that Will Jordan had been involved with at any one time but knew there were probably many, many more.

We became a source of comfort to each other as gradually our conversations moved from talking about him to just talking about life in general – how our kids were, what we were working on, normal stuff. It was a fledgling community of support and understanding, helping us all to heal.

WET CEMENT

The public response to the book was very different to the victim-shaming reaction to the newspaper articles. People started to leave reviews online saying the book had really opened their eyes to how easily a psychopath can manipulate someone. I started to get letters through my publisher and online from people thanking me for writing it. I started a Facebook page and people started to comment on that too. More and more people said something similar had happened to them and they had not felt they could speak out about it until they had read my book, thanking me for coming forward. It was extraordinarily validating.

However, not everyone was positive. One friend whom I had known for many years and helped through her own traumas had been a great support to me at one of my lowest points. She had come round for coffee one day in April 2006, just a few days after I'd found out the truth, and found me in an old and very baggy T-shirt which was slightly torn. She berated me, telling me to look after myself no matter what was happening and not to let myself go. It gave me a little emotional slap and I duly took a little more care after that to ensure that I wasn't slipping too far into depression. However, when she found out that I was talking to the children about what was happening she was totally incensed that I had even chosen to tell them the truth at all. She felt that I should have lied to them and let them grow up idolising a dead or absent father, or just tell them nothing at all. She actually said to me that telling the children the truth was 'tantamount to child abuse', and then she refused to speak to me again.

I knew that she was wrong. Being open and talking about things with my children was the right thing to do. I was giving them the language and tools to express how they felt and not bottle things up. I wanted to give them the chance to understand what they were feeling and explore what that meant.

By 2007 my eldest daughter, Robyn, was already showing signs of 'separation anxiety', unsurprisingly. At only eight years old she had already lost three of the four most important people in her life – all in the space of a single year – and she was terrified of losing me as well.

In January 2006 her biological father, Ross, had married a lovely Japanese lady and in March he moved to Japan. Robyn hadn't seen him much before he left; once or twice a month he would turn up and take her out.

I had stopped telling her in advance that he might be coming to see her when she was about four because he would arrange it, and then go out drinking the night before and just not show up (or cancel last minute). He didn't have to deal with her little sad face each time. I had to tell her the trip to the zoo was cancelled or the cinema outing was off. It became easier to just have him turn up as a surprise (when he did).

He never supported her financially and I eventually stopped pushing the issue because I felt her relationship with her father was more important and we clearly weren't going to get any financial support anyway.

So in January 2006 I had wanted Ross to tell Robyn that he was moving to Japan, but although he promised to, he just never did. I finally had to tell her myself, two weeks before he left. She wasn't particularly bothered but it was just the first 'hit' of the year.

Robyn adored Will Jordan. He had been her stepfather since she was a one-year-old baby, and made a big fuss of her whenever he was home. They played games and he would pick her up and swing her around. To her he was far more of a 'father' than Ross had ever been.

When the truth of what Will Jordan had done emerged, Robyn was only seven years old and in the second year of primary school. When I made the decision to talk to the children, I told her and Eilidh everything that was going on, including the fact that he was in jail. Robyn took the news that Will Jordan was married to someone else on the chin and seemed to understand that he was in jail because that was where he should be after committing a crime.

When Robyn's school peers heard the news, they tried to use it against her – as children often do – but she already knew and so didn't react.

They taunted her with, 'Your dad's in jail!'

She just shrugged and replied, 'Yes . . . And?'

It stopped them in their tracks because they didn't get the reaction they wanted. I was so proud of her.

It was a tough few months but we got through it day by day together.

Then her lovely grandmother died. The three most important adults (other than me) in Robyn's life were gone within six months of each other. She had been deserted, betrayed and bereaved, the trilogy of hurt, all at the age of seven years old.

Robyn was terrified that I was going to disappear too. Whenever I dropped her off at school she would become anxious that I wouldn't be there to pick her up again. I had to stand and wave as she walked past two separate windows, and I had to be in the same exact spot to greet her once school was over. Whenever I went away to do a TV interview or promote the book she worried that the plane I was travelling in would crash and/or that I just wouldn't come back.

I felt so bad for her, to lose so much at such a vulnerable age. We just kept talking through it all. I told her how I felt about things and she told me how she felt, and gradually we grew stronger together.

As my three children grew up, I wondered if there was any chance that psychopathy was genetic. I read a book called *Just Like His Father?* by Dr Liane Leedom. It was fascinating and did indeed show that psychopathy can be passed from parent to child but that the environment, how a child is brought up, also matters. A child might have a predisposition for psychopathy but doesn't have to turn into a psychopath even if they have no chemical empathic response. I learnt that it is important to watch out for tendencies towards antisocial behaviour so I could take action to counteract it quickly if it occurred. Being aware and informed is the key. So is teaching them a strong moral code – in my case the most basic of principles, that lying was not only wrong but completely unacceptable. So I watched for signs of psychopathy in my children. However, it was clear relatively quickly that my children all had emotional response and empathy for others which was a massive relief. Being aware and keeping my eyes open made me feel more in control.

I'm not saying that being a single parent was all plain sailing. There were (and still are) huge challenges in being a parent, not least having to do everything myself. Generally I just got on with it and didn't think how much I had to do but I remember one incident that brought my situation into sharp focus.

My lovely friend Mandy came to stay with me for a few weeks because she was between jobs and flats. It was an absolutely delight to have her there and although she thought I was doing her a favour by putting her up, in fact it was the complete opposite. She was doing me the favour just by being there to provide me with company. Being another woman, she just got on with things that needed doing like tidying up or making the children something to eat. I remember the first day she was there very clearly. I had just finished bathing the children and getting them ready for bed and Mandy had tidied the kitchen and done the washing up. More than that, she had heated up Zach's bedtime bottle. I burst into tears. It might sound ridiculous but at the time I had no one to do anything around the house but me, so even that small gesture was enormous to me. It was lovely having Mandy live with us and I think it really kept me sane over those difficult early months.

I cried buckets when Mandy moved into her own place, though I made sure she didn't know at the time. Obviously she had to move on with her own life but I missed having her around for adult company as well as for all the help she had given me. (Even though she now has three children of her own, I still jokingly ask her to marry me every so often.)

My mother had once given me a huge piece of advice about my children – she reminded me that they are adults far longer than they are children and that I would want to have a relationship with them long beyond them reaching maturity. My job was to get them to adulthood strong, confident, self-sufficient individuals who were ready to face the world, and by the time they were adults to see them as equals.

I knew that in the end children will always copy what we do, rather than what we say, so we have to teach our children by example. I had decided that however I reacted to the situation with Will Jordan I was showing my children how to deal with adversity, and ultimately I could choose to let it destroy me or make me stronger and launch me into something new. Which of these two options did I want to teach my children? If in the future one of them came to me with a similar problem, what would I advise them to do? Because whatever I did was setting that benchmark and showing them the way.

I can't remember where I heard it but I also remember someone saying that children are like wet cement, because anything that falls on them makes an impression. So I decided that this was a golden opportunity to teach them never to let the world beat them down and always to rise up again no matter what happens to you.

Jon Ronson

The best media show, and the most enduring, had to be my interview with Jon Ronson in 2007. Jon is an investigative journalist and BBC Radio 4 presenter, as well as the bestselling author of books like *Them: Adventures with Extremists* and *The Men Who Stare at Goats*. He invited me for interview in a London studio, for a six-minute segment for a thirty-minute radio show. His new series was going to have a different theme for each programme and this one was about people waking up after being conned.

It seems strange to think that I would travel all the way from Edinburgh to London for a six-minute interview but that was all part of the job. I was promoting my book but also sharing my knowledge with a wider audience and hopefully protecting people from falling into similar relationships. Little would I know at the time how big an impact that single interview would have!

We sat down to start recording (it would be edited later) and discussed the story chronologically. Jon seemed genuinely fascinated and even wondered at one point if Will Jordan had indeed been in the CIA because otherwise, how could he have done some of the things he had, or known ahead of time things that would come out on the news?

'You don't have to know how a magic trick is done to know that it's not real magic,' I replied.

Two hours later Jon was still quizzing me about my story and one aspect really shook him.

I calmly said, 'I was kept pregnant and kept tired and kept stressed, and I was basically in a state of fear for six years. And things that you look back on rationally now, you realise . . . that just doesn't make sense. That's all part of the plan. If you keep somebody stressed, tired and in distress then they don't think rationally, especially if they can't talk about it.'

'Why are you OK with this?' he asked. 'Why aren't you a total wreck?'

'Because it's not personal,' I shrugged. I was passing it off nonchalantly, but in fact his question made me realise how far I'd really come. I felt strong and knowledgeable. It made me feel powerful.

'I can't think of anything MORE personal!' Jon exclaimed.

'Will Jordan is a psychopath and psychopaths don't behave that way because of anything their victim has done. It's like a lion chasing a zebra, or a cat chasing a mouse. The cat doesn't choose the mouse because it's pretty or rich, or whether it's intelligent, kind or even if it has babies or not. It is all just about the cat and its game. I see Will as a predator; I don't see him as a human being any more. The only way I can describe it is that you can watch a tiger attacking an antelope or a zebra without resenting or being angry with the tiger. It is just in the nature of the predator and the hunter to hunt. And if the zebra managed to escape and get away with its life, it wouldn't actually be offended by what had happened to it. It would be relieved to get away.'

Jon was really taken aback and so stunned to think that there were people in the world who are like lions in society. Predators treating the rest of us like prey. He decided to make the whole of his first episode about my story and called it *The Internet Date from Hell*.

Our episode of his radio show came third in the Sony Awards that year and has been aired over and over again in the last twelve years.

Jon didn't stop there though. He went on to research and find out more about sociopaths and psychopaths. He wrote another book called *The Psychopath Test* in 2011. Although he didn't mention our meeting in the book itself, he did credit me with inspiring him to write it in an interview he gave to the *Guardian* newspaper, saying:

'I don't put it in the book, but I met a woman called Mary Turner Thomson. In fact I made a radio documentary about her . . . Two things really struck me about the story. First, when I asked her if she felt hurt by him, she said, "No, he's a sociopath. It's not personal. Does the wildebeest take it personally when it's being chased by the lion? No. It's their nature." And, second, I talked to a Harvard psychologist named Martha Stout who said that his condition – psychopathy, or sociopathy, or whatever you want to call it – is prevalent in the rulers of our world. The wars, the economic injustice, she said; a great deal of it is initiated by sociopaths. Their brain anomaly is so powerful it has remoulded society all wrong. This struck me as such a huge thought, I kept wondering if I could verify it. Could I become a professional psychopath spotter and journey into the corridors of power?'

The Psychopath Test was rightly a huge success for Jon and still sells very well.

The interview with Jon really felt like a turning point to me. I felt empowered and that I really knew what I was talking about. Jon's easy-going and relaxed interviewing technique allowed me to articulate things in a way that I hadn't before, and solidified ideas in my head. I left the studio feeling that something new had been born and that I had made it back to normality.

EDINBURGH BOOK FESTIVAL

One of the main highlights of being an author is being asked to attend book festivals, and to me the golden ticket is being invited to speak at the Edinburgh International Book Festival. Something I had visited year in and year out and that my mother had looked forward to every year. I was delighted to be asked in August 2008 to speak about my book *The Bigamist* and even more so to be able to go into the illustrious Authors' Yurt. There I was surrounded by all the other authors presenting at the festival and I was fan-girling like crazy, all the while trying to look nonchalant and like I belonged. I was hobnobbing around the pastries with celebrities like Jacqueline Wilson, Kate Mosse and Terry Pratchett. Even Sean Connery made an appearance.

Being allowed to use the Authors' Yurt throughout the whole of the Edinburgh Book Festival (and not just on your own event day) is a huge perk of being asked to speak. I made as much use of it as possible. One day I was there to see Ian Rankin speak and popped into the yurt beforehand for a drink. I stood at the table which was laid out with all manner of drinks – from coffee and tea, to whisky and wine, as well as a feast of croissants and sandwiches and cakes. Several people joined me and we all started to chat. One of the authors started talking about his difficulties in getting a babysitter. He talked about how he'd asked everyone he could think of and ended up getting some random Spanish woman to do it.

I laughed and said, 'It's funny, isn't it?' as he looked at me quizzically. 'I mean, we spend our whole lives telling our children to be wary of strangers and then we pay them to come into our homes.'

He looked horrified and then exclaimed he was just about to go onstage and I had now put *that* in his head. He was not pleased.

That was when I realised it was Ian Rankin I was speaking to.

'Sorry,' I said.

My event was on 19 August 2008, two years after my mother's death and my first workshops at the Edinburgh Book Festival at the start of my writing journey. My event was sold out and I spent two hours afterwards signing books and talking to people who wanted to ask a private question or just get a photograph with me.

After that I was feeling very full of myself and went for a wander around the bookshop tent at the Festival. I picked up a couple of books I wanted to buy and went to stand in the queue. There in front of me stood a woman holding *The Bigamist*. I was still feeling pretty cocky and so I tapped her cheerfully on the shoulder and said, 'That's my book. Do you want me to sign it for you?'

She turned and looked me up and down with disdain before simply replying with a flat 'No'.

I was mortified and wanted the ground to swallow me up – but pride rooted me to the spot and I had to stand behind her for another full five minutes until we were served. Afterwards, I realised how insane a situation that must have been for the woman. I must have looked like a complete nutter tapping her on the shoulder in a bookshop queue. The last thing you expect when buying a book is to have the author standing behind you like some kind of weird literary stalker.

I imagine that she went home and opened up the book to see my photograph and then went, 'Oh!'

WORK AND LOVE

Now the book was out, the issue of what work I should do was starting to become clear. I knew I wanted to be available for my children before and after school as well as during the school holidays so the best answer was to work with the schools system itself.

I did an Open University course (and eventually got another degree) in English & Creative Writing. I started doing author visits to schools, and also created a programme which took classes of students (usually aged between nine and thirteen) through the process of creating characters, setting scenes and writing storylines. The programme started small but developed a good reputation over time. I absolutely love working with children as they have immense imaginations and the ability to come up with stories and endings that just wouldn't occur to adults.

I started to get a bit frustrated though. All these wonderful stories we created were just evaporating after I left each school. Having known what it feels like to become a published author I initially thought that I would like my own three children to have the opportunity to feel like that, but then I realised I was thinking too small and wanted *all* children to feel like that.

So I decided to start my own publishing company, a company that specifically published the stories and books that the children came up with on the programme. Because I was initially published by a company called Mainstream Publishing, I called my own company WhiteWater Publishing, really as rather a joke.

The interactive and fun workshops extended to writing, publishing and marketing books – all showcasing the children's amazingly creative ideas and often illustrated by the students themselves. It was a great success. The children saw their work in print and as a consequence started to look at all books in a new light. More than that though, the teachers had a showcase of the type of work the children were doing, and the parents had a keepsake of their children's work. The school had books they could sell to raise money. It was a win/win situation for everyone involved.

I didn't know how to publish books, I'd had no experience of this at all, but I knew I had the capacity to learn. I simply started out and learnt as I went along. How to do the design and layout of books, new software I could use, and how the industry worked. Interestingly enough, it was finding the competitive commercial printers that proved to be the most challenging. In the end though, I learnt bit by bit and within a fairly short space of time found it was not as complicated as I had initially thought.

Finally I had a means of earning money again, and a job that allowed me to work during school hours so that I was always available for my children. I didn't make a huge income but it was at least better than being on government benefits.

Things were moving on for me. Physically, I was getting stronger and better at taekwondo and becoming more confident in my ability to defend myself. Financially, I was earning an income again as an author and publisher. Mentally, my self-esteem and self-confidence was being rebuilt through my research and ability to talk to people about a subject I was now becoming fluent in. But emotionally I was still not ready to think about another romantic relationship. The idea of having another man in my life did not appeal – even looking past the awkward aspect of having to date again and find someone who would be interested in a single mother of three young children – I did not want another person to tidy up after or wash their socks! I already had enough to do.

However, I had got to the stage that I wanted some emotional support as well as feeling that my children needed another living creature to love other than just me. After thinking long and hard about it, I decided to get a dog.

My sisters thought I was mad and on paper it does sound like just another mouth to feed and another body to look after. I was determined though and even moved house from the fairly comfortable flat we had been living in to a small flat with a garden because the new landlord would allow us to have a puppy.

I researched it quite carefully and although none of my children were allergic to dogs, I didn't know if any of their friends would be. I decided to get a cockapoo because they don't shed and so don't trigger allergies. I wanted to make sure the dog wasn't from a puppy farm, so I looked for one from a genuine home. I found a family in Sheffield that had just had a litter of cockapoos, and started to get photographs of my dog from the time she was born. As we waited the weeks until she was ready to come to her new adoptive home our excitement grew. We decided to call her 'Honey', partly because she is honey-coloured and partly so that when I walked in the door I could say, 'Hi, Honey, I'm home!'

The day finally came and I travelled by train down to Sheffield, where the family met me at the station. The tiny ball of beige fluff was handed over to me and I instantly fell in love. The feeling quickly became mutual. All the way home on the train people came up to say hello. Honey was just too cute to pass without wanting to pat her.

She was so adorable as a puppy that when I would go to collect my kids from school, I would be surrounded by hordes of children wanting to stroke her fur. She grew into the most loving and lovely creature you could possibly want. A dog so devoted and sweet that she has become my constant companion, the love of my life and adored by my children. She follows me everywhere and gives me the most wonderful affectionate cuddles. If anyone were to threaten me or my family she would race to defend us, and I know she would never do anything to hurt or upset me. She is the ideal partner and what's more, I don't have to wash her socks!

GET OUT OF JAIL – FREE

I remember very clearly standing in my kitchen talking again on the phone to Victim Support in early 2009. I wanted reassurance that Will Jordan was still in jail and to find out how to petition to have him deported on his release. I had talked to numerous people by that stage and asked repeatedly what was going to happen without any definitive answer. The uncertainty was unnerving. Having told the whole world what he'd done to me and others, I was not certain how Will Jordan would respond once he got out of jail. Would he come looking for me and seek to punish me? Would he try to seduce me and suck me back under his control again? I was very anxious about both options. I also didn't know how the children would react if he turned up out of the blue.

I worried daily that he might have been released early without my knowledge and that he could kidnap my young children and take them away. The other wife had told me several times that if anything happened to me, she would look after my children along with her own, which I found particularly disturbing. What if Will Jordan took my two younger children to her? Would the police even help me if he was their genetic father?

Only a few weeks earlier there had been an event when I couldn't find ten-year-old Robyn after school. It had been one of the worst hours of my life. With mounting panic I'd asked teachers and school friends in the playground but no one knew where she was. I freaked out, thinking it was possible that Will Jordan had taken her or that he had arranged for someone else to kidnap her. There was a remote possibility that she had gone home alone, so I dashed between the school and the flat with my two younger children in tow, looking for her. She wasn't at home. Frantic, I left the two younger kids with my neighbour with instructions to call me if she appeared, and ran full pelt back to the school. I was desperately clinging to the thought that Will Jordan was still in jail and it was far more likely that something mundane had happened. But my history with him haunted me and added an extra layer of panic. Back at the school the teachers rallied around and one remembered seeing Robyn with one of the other students and their mum at the gates so they called the mother. To my incredible relief, it turned out that the mother (someone Robyn knew well) had invited her over for a play date and said she would text to tell me but had forgotten to do so! I was not best pleased but recognised that the mother had not meant to cause me so much worry and it was a simple mistake.

Gripping the phone tightly, I heard the man from Victim Support say, 'He's going to be deported straight from jail back to the USA.' I breathed a sigh of relief as he continued, 'His legal wife divorced him in jail and he won't be allowed to return to the UK . . . ever.'

It was the best news I had ever heard. I had been so worried about what was going to happen once he was released and free to do whatever he liked again. I felt like the huge weight that had been hanging over me for three years had suddenly lifted. Feeling like my entire country was behind me and telling this man he was not allowed to come back to the UK released me from my prison of anxiety over him.

A few weeks later on 29 April 2009, Will Jordan (at forty-four years old) was issued a passport for three days only. It was stamped with 'VALID

FOR DIRECT TRAVEL TO THE UNITED STATES ONLY' by the American Embassy in London. On 2 May 2009, he was duly taken from prison in England and put on a plane back to New Jersey, USA, with only the clothes he had been wearing when arrested. I can only assume he went back to his parents' house in Cherry Hill.

For my little family it was such a huge relief. I didn't have to look over my shoulder or worry about what he might do to the children just to manipulate or hurt me. He was out of the country. I knew it was not the end though, just the start of a new chapter, and it would only be a matter of time before I would be contacted by new victims.

OLD TRICKS

Seven months later I got the first of the emails I had been expecting in November 2009, from a woman who had been left pregnant and homeless. I immediately wrote back and we talked on the phone. She told me what had happened to her.

Within a week of being deported back to the USA, Will Jordan had joined at least one dating site and met a new victim. As a single mother in her early thirties she had tried to be very careful about who she met online and so when she was contacted by a calm and stable man she felt assured he would be a good match. The man was thirty-nine years old, called Will Allen and he had just arrived back from the UK. She had a lot of empathy for this man because he had had such a hard life. As a child he'd been severely abused by his mother, and his father had initially sent him to Canada as a toddler to prevent his mother abusing him further. After that he was adopted by British relatives in Oxford and got an education there. He stayed in Oxford to get his doctorate and then got a job working for the FCO (Foreign & Commonwealth Office). The FCO posted him to Tokyo, where he went with 'M' (Will Jordan's nickname for a girlfriend whom he once referred to as Megan). 'M' had betrayed him though and had cheated on him, getting pregnant and having another man's baby. He complained that 'M' had destroyed his life and almost ruined his career, so he went back to the UK and then finally came back to the USA to work for both the FCO and Barclays Bank. He had decided to come to terms with his mother, who by that stage was extremely sick and dying. Will Allen hated his parents but felt he needed to lay the ghosts to rest.

As a result of his experiences with his mother he had not had many relationships and not a lot of experience with women. He had never married and had no children.

Will Allen wrote long beautiful emails, had great manners, great conversation and was a fluent flatterer. He seemed very kind and loving with her child. He was excellent in bed, a good cook, and polite to all her friends, neighbours and even her ex-husband. He just seemed like the perfect man.

Once she got to know him better, she found out he was being called to serve as the Financial Attaché for the British Embassy in Washington. Plus he had a role working for Barclays Bank as the Director of Co-operative Strategies in the UK and had been asked to develop a similar team in the USA and Latin America within the next three years. She even saw his passport in the name of Will Allen, which was stamped by the American Embassy in London with some illegible text and the words 'Diplomatic Attaché' on it.

In June 2009 they discovered she was pregnant. Will Allen was delighted to be having his 'first' child and they decided to move in together. As their relationship progressed everything was going well but then things started to get a bit weird. Bills were not being paid and money started to get tight. Then money went missing from her relatively healthy bank account. Whilst she was trying to sort that out, Will Allen persuaded her to move into a new home with him and went to sign the papers. They had packed up all their belongings (mostly hers) into a van and she and her child drove it to the new house. However, there was someone already living there, and the person in the house knew nothing about selling the place and sent her packing. The real estate agent didn't know anything about it either. Also, there was no answer from Will Allen's phone and she had no other way of contacting him.

Finally, confused and worried, she checked her bank accounts and found that $10,000 was missing. She told me he had cashed a cheque leaving a different name on the details – the name William Allen Jordan. She immediately looked the name up online and to her horror found my website and photographs of him.

She was stunned.

She went to the police but they didn't think a crime had been committed and so told her there was nothing they could do. Then she sent me an email.

We spoke at length and I found her to be an intelligent caring woman who was completely shaken by what had happened. At first she was frightened that he would come after her after finding out his true identity, but her fear quickly turned to anger. Finally she decided to move away altogether and get away from him and the situation. She decided not to stay in touch with me and to bring up her children with no knowledge of Will Jordan – which of course is her choice. I told her that the door is always open to her.

◆ ◆ ◆

The next two victims came in quick succession in December 2009, with very similar stories to the last. They had all overlapped with each other. Each time, Will Jordan had met the women online, seduced them and promised a life together, taken money, then left them high and dry. He had told them that he was working for the British Foreign Office. He even showed them his passport and birth certificate, both of which now stated his name was William Allen and that he was born in 1970. (His actual date of birth is 22 May 1965.) He was passing himself off as British, or American-born but raised in the UK by foster parents (or an academic aunt). He told stories of childhood abuse by a mother who threw him down the stairs, or previous partners who had physically abused him. His stories repeated patterns that revolved around similar themes.

He was definitely up to his old tricks again and showed no sign of slowing down.

Mind Games, Megan's Law and Physical Confidence

Once deported, Will Jordan got back in touch with his ex-wife in the UK. She was still calling me regularly and we talked on the phone two or three times a week. She told me he had been in touch and wanted her to go to America with the children to be with him again. She clearly felt the tug but talking it through with me seemed to settle her a bit.

Once she called me in an excited state. She had just been contacted by Will Jordan's psychiatrist in the USA who was treating him for pathological lying.

'He's finally sought treatment and wants to get better,' she said, talking rapidly and in a slightly high-pitched voice. 'The psychiatrist wanted to talk to me to ascertain what's true, so he can best treat Bill's pathology. We talked for over an hour about his treatment and what Bill is doing to recover. He really wants to be cured.'

'Take a breath,' I said, 'and keep calm. You need to take a step back.'

I knew this routine well, and I knew to be suspicious of basic principles of anything connected to this man.

'Firstly,' I said, 'a psychiatrist would never, NEVER call someone's ex-wife to verify anything their patient said. It would be totally unethical and against all their rules. So the only logical conclusion is that the person who called you was actually Will Jordan himself.'

She quickly realised I was right. It couldn't possibly be anyone else. She described this 'psychiatrist' as having a strong American accent and a very different voice to Will. I advised her not to entertain him because there was no benefit to doing so but she decided to string him along. She spoke to the 'psychiatrist' again for a couple of hours and noticed that his accent started to slip. The 'psychiatrist' tried to lay the groundwork for him to suck her back into his life but knowing it was him made her realise what he was doing. She was not swayed. Realising the ploy was not working the 'psychiatrist' didn't call her again.

Another time she called me in a frantic voice and said, 'He's dead! He's been shot.'

To some degree I would not be surprised if some victim, or member of a victim's family had cracked and decided to end Will Jordan's life. However, I was now conditioned not to react nor believe anything that was not proven and externally verified when it was about him. So without even a momentary flinch, I replied, 'How do you know. Who told you?'

She went on to tell me that her eldest son had been told by Will's adopted sister that he'd been shot and killed the previous day. The other wife had sat her children down and told them and then called me.

'Is there anyone that can verify it? Anyone you know that you can call?'

'I can talk to his uncle,' she said.

'OK. Do that, then call me back,' I said.

Ten minutes later she was back, much quieter and rather subdued. 'He's not dead,' she said simply. 'His uncle saw him alive and well this morning.'

I'm not sure what he was trying to achieve by informing her he was dead. I suspect it was to stop me/us from paying attention to what he was doing, or maybe it was just to continue manipulating her and their children. Maybe it was just an impulsive act designed only to mess with his ex-wife's mind again. One thing seemed clear though, he still had people helping him.

◆ ◆ ◆

When Will Jordan was deported, I got in touch with the New Jersey State Police in 2009 to inform them that a convicted sex offender was now living there and should be registered under Megan's Law. This law states that no matter where you have been convicted of a sexual offence, you must be registered as an offender when living in the USA.

This is the online register in the USA for all sex offenders which was sparked into existence after seven-year-old Megan Kanka was kidnapped, raped and murdered by her neighbour in May 1997. Her parents said they would never have let her play outside if they had known their neighbour was a convicted sex offender (he had lured her into his house to meet his new puppy). That statement sparked a nationwide outcry and led to Megan's Law being passed, requiring communities to be notified when a sex offender moves into the neighbourhood.

The woman I spoke to at the New Jersey State Police said that Will Jordan's case was not relevant because they interpreted that to mean 'no matter where in the *USA* you have been convicted'. She told me that different countries have different laws, and something that might be considered a 'sexual offence' in Saudi Arabia might not be considered a sexual offence in the USA. Aghast, I said that British law was not that different to USA law and that he was a convicted paedophile for sexual offences against a girl under the age of thirteen! The police officer just shrugged me off, saying that was the law.

I even talked to Interpol, and the policeman who dealt with Will Jordan's bigamy case in the UK, and asked them to contact the New Jersey police, but had no luck.

As it turns out, the New Jersey State police officer was wrong. In 2008, the law had changed to encompass anyone convicted of sex offences in the USA, UK, Canada and Australia. If they moved to America they had to be registered along with everyone convicted in the USA.

It was incredibly frustrating knowing there was a sexual predator and psychopath roaming around the USA, one that *should* by law have to register his address to help protect the children and communities around him. Although I had met with dead end after dead end, I wasn't going to give up. This wouldn't be the end of the story.

◆ ◆ ◆

Over the years I had taken taekwondo gradings at every opportunity and was now a black stripe belt (one stage from black belt). Then one day, my physical confidence was tested as I walked the dog with my two eldest children in tow.

It was a sunny Friday afternoon and school was finished for the day. My young son was still at nursery so I was walking the dog in a city park, with my now ten-year-old Robyn and seven-year-old Eilidh. We noticed a group of eight teenagers, between fifteen and eighteen years old, mostly boys, smoking and talking as they leaned against the wall of a primary school.

I noticed a small stack of leaves and sticks burning up against the wall of the school some yards away from them and asked if it was theirs, thinking the fire might have been started by a discarded cigarette butt by accident. There had been a spate of 'fire-starting' in Edinburgh recently and I was aware it was something to be careful of. The teenagers all shook their heads, so I went and stamped it out.

As soon as I had finished and started to walk away one of the teenagers started walking over, striking at a box of matches as they went back to the site of the now dead bonfire.

'Oh, so it *is* your bonfire,' I said, taking out my mobile phone to call the police as I continued to walk away.

'She's gonnae call the polis!' said one of the teenagers.

I had a better thought though, and turned towards them pretending to take photos. (Funnily enough, my phone didn't have that facility!) It was like I had dropped a grenade on the group. Five out of the eight teenagers ran away. Honey, my now one-year-old cockapoo, thinking it a great game, barked in a frenzy and ran with them. The runners screamed and ran faster, thinking they were being chased. The other three pulled up their hoodies and squared up.

The leader of the gang started to yell threats at me. He made the shape of a gun with both hands and gestured one point up and the other down. I had only ever seen something like it on TV. He was obviously trying to look like a 'hard man' as he growled, 'I'm going to MESS you UP!'

I felt remarkably calm. I regularly had to defend myself against four other black belts (all at the same time) whilst we trained, and I could easily hold my own. I also knew that I would never let a man, let alone a teenager, try to intimidate me mentally or physically again.

'Oh,' I said, unconcerned, 'really?', making sure my daughters were behind me. I wasn't going to let them be scared.

'Aye,' he added, 'I'm gonnae f*ck you up!'

I started casually walking towards him and his two friends who were now standing behind him.

'Well,' I said, taking a step forward, 'you have to consider two things.'

'What's that then?' he said, slightly nonplussed that I wasn't scared.

'Firstly, how big are you going to look, trying to beat up a forty-year-old woman? And secondly . . .' I took another couple of steps forward so that I was standing right in front of him, nose to nose. 'You have to consider that you MIGHT . . . NOT . . . WIN!'

At this point the teenager looked scared and shrank away. I can't take all the credit though because as all this was going on, Robyn, my eldest daughter, was tugging at my jacket loudly and frantically repeating, 'Mum, Mum! Don't hurt him, Mum! Don't hurt him.'

I love the fact that my daughter had so much faith in my ability not only to defend us but also to do damage. I think it was as much her confidence in me rather than my own that made him back down.

My dog returned, wagging her tail and we walked away from that scenario, hopefully having made those teenagers think twice about their actions, but probably not. However, my daughters learnt not to be scared and that physical confidence matters.

I trained hard at taekwondo and was very focused on getting my black belt. It's not an easy thing to do but it helped me focus on not just surviving but building up my confidence again. Each grading challenged me and pushed me forward, step by step. Yellow belt, green belt, blue belt, red belt with striped belts in between. Each grade meaning more skill, more strength, more power and more control. I had to study to learn Korean terms and commands as well as the history and meaning of each pattern. It is not just a physical sport, it is mental training as well. There are five tenets to live by – courtesy, integrity, perseverance, self-control and indomitable spirit. I believed in them all and taught them to my children. As well as that, the people I trained with had now become like family, all of them younger than me and mostly men.

The black belt exam was extraordinary. Not only did I have to demonstrate all the patterns and sit a written exam but I also had to spar one-on-one with another black belt. Then I had to spar against two black belts, and then three. Finally I had to demonstrate that I could defend myself from an attack by four other black belts. You can see why a group of three unskilled teenagers seemed like a fairly easy option!

The children had all started doing taekwondo as well and were showing great promise. It was great we could all do a sport together rather than with the other clubs they did such as dancing or football where I had to just stand and watch, or wait outside until they'd finished. It was also proving useful to them all in life. It helped Robyn with her separation anxiety. Eilidh had several occasions where she had stopped incidences of children bullying others in the playground simply by walking up to the aggressors – who were often much older than her – and telling them to stop. And Zach had already been doing taekwondo for a couple of years by the time he started school. There was a boy in his class who used to physically bully the other boys but he gave Zach and his friends a wide berth. Zach was even given a commendation by the school for sticking up for a little girl his peers were upsetting.

Getting my black belt was a hugely important moment. I am still proud of it today. I thoroughly recommend it to anyone who has been victimised in any way or even just to help boost self-confidence. Doing taekwondo (or any other martial art) is not just about fighting. It is a community of people; it is fitness, strength, friendship and defence, all wrapped up in a boost to physical confidence. It was something I really needed at that time and it made a huge difference to my life.

MEXICO

Another year rolled by and another shocked victim contacted me from Mexico. It was 2010. Juan was very worried about his sister as she was currently in a relationship with Will Jordan and Juan had only just discovered his real identity. He told me that Will Jordan had not only lured his sister, but had ruined his whole family financially. Juan asked if I would talk to his sister and help her break free from him. I agreed immediately and tentatively reached out to Amabel, who told me her whole story.

Amabel, a Mexican national, worked with Down's Syndrome children. At twenty-three years old she joined a dating site because she'd heard lots of stories about happy couples who had met online and wanted to find a happy and healthy relationship too. Her family didn't know anything about it but she thought she would just try it out. Almost immediately she was contacted by a man called Bill Jones. He seemed to be nice and said he'd not had a lot of experience with relationships, just like Amabel. Bill was extremely polite, seemed very kind and was quite charming and willing to help. From the very beginning Bill talked about marriage and settling down together.

Here was a tall, dark handsome man from Britain who worked for a well-known British bank. He said he was thirty-six (nine years younger than he actually was, at forty-five).

The emails were long and fluent, and although Amabel felt that this man was probably a little old for her there was a huge feeling that they just 'clicked'. The conversation flowed between them and they seemed to have so much in common.

Very quickly they started to talk on the phone and again, Amabel was very comfortable with him. He said such lovely things and made her feel really special. Everything was so perfect that she felt she had found her one unique person.

He asked her to come to the USA to meet up but Amabel suggested instead that he come to Mexico, so he dropped everything and went south.

The first few days after he arrived were perfect. He was everything he had promised to be: polite, attentive, kind and such a loving man. Amabel felt so cared about and loved. Bill Jones seemed to have money to burn and was spending it lavishly on her. He lived in a hotel and wanted her to move in with him as soon as possible.

Part of his luggage had been retained by customs staff, together with a couple of his credit cards and he had to wait about two weeks to get them back.

Bill promised they would make a life together and he would set up home in Mexico with her. Within a week of him moving to Mexico, Amabel decided to move in with him. It was far faster than she would usually have moved but it felt like such a whirlwind romance and she had a strong sense of 'when it's right, it's right'. So she packed up her stuff and moved into his hotel suite.

He told her he had plenty of money and a good job with Barclays Bank, and his office were prepared to let him relocate. A man called Alex Armitage telephoned and spoke to Amabel when Bill was out – he appeared to have a very British accent and came across as extremely camp on the phone. Alex left a message for Bill saying he was now in charge of his relocation and would be the contact for anything to do with the move. Alex phoned a few times and left messages or spoke to Amabel about the problems they were having in setting up bank accounts, and passed on details for Bill and the relocation. Everything would get sorted out very soon, he said, and she had to hang on tight and wait a bit longer.

Bill showed Amabel a bank account statement which showed he had at least $500,000 in his account but said he simply couldn't get access to it at that time. In the meantime, Bill asked Amabel to set up a bank account in her name for him. Amabel agreed and proceeded to try to do that, but the bank kept holding things up and making mistakes.

Almost immediately after Amabel had moved into Bill's suite, he suggested that they start looking for an apartment of their own to live together.

They found an apartment quite quickly and Amabel had to sign all the paperwork because Bill was not Mexican and didn't have a residence permit; everything had to go under Amabel's name. Bill paid the deposit by online transfer which somehow never appeared, so he paid them a check for $3,000 instead, signed in the name of Will Jones.

Very soon after Amabel moved in, the money issues started. Bill had tried to move bank accounts and told her that his original bank account had been set up but was blocked and the new account was not opened yet. He claimed there were incompetent people at his office who were responsible for slow transfers and wrong digits on accounts. All the ways that Bill would usually get cash suddenly dried up and the money he had on cards was inaccessible.

Amabel started to pay for things herself from her salary. It wasn't enough though. They needed more money to make ends meet and so Amabel borrowed 30,000 pesos from her mother to tide them over. For the next three weeks Amabel managed to keep them afloat.

Meanwhile, Bill decided to leave the bank and set up a restaurant in Mexico. However, he needed help to set up the business and hired Amabel's brother, Juan, to assist him. Things always seemed just about to get back on track and Bill even suggested that he and Amabel go on holiday together. He asked her to give him her passport, birth certificate and other documents from her school so he could buy tickets and they could go on holiday in October 2010.

After a short time, Juan decided something was very wrong. Bill had no money to pay him, nor to buy anything for the restaurant. Bill said that his passport and wallet had been stolen which had delayed things further. Juan started to investigate. He stayed back at the hotel one day when Bill and Amabel went out and searched through everything that Bill possessed. He found nothing incriminating but Juan couldn't shake the suspicious feeling.

Then one day Bill left his backpack behind and Juan looked through it. Inside he found documents, a dozen credit cards under different names, and two passports, one fraudulent and one under the name of William Allen Jordan. He looked the name up on the Internet and was horrified to see pictures, articles and information about this international con man and serial sexual predator.

That was when Juan looked me up and contacted me by email, asking if I would talk to his sister. I agreed immediately and she and I started to talk. Amabel was very shaken but I explained that it was nothing she had done, nor had she deserved to be treated this way. I let her tell me her story and helped her to see along each step of the way what was true and (mostly) what was not.

Amabel's family rallied around and took her out of the hotel that night, leaving behind all her belongings, including her computer, her clothes and documents.

Initially Amabel told Will that she had family problems and would be back with him shortly. Then she spoke to the hotel owner and arranged to pick up her stuff when Will was out. She got everything except her passport and birth certificate which Will Jordan had in a file in his backpack.

Amabel went to Interpol and the police but no one was interested and they just sent her away. Finally a police officer took an interest in the fact that Will Jordan still had her passport and thought they could arrest him for theft, but as soon as the police were involved Will Jordan disappeared. Amabel received her documents back by post.

Will Jordan initially called and texted Amabel to try to talk her round. He promised that he had his reasons for doing what he had done and everything was not as it seemed. He even promised to send proof but it was never forthcoming.

The whole relationship with Will lasted just over a month but the devastation Amabel feels will last a lifetime. The first few weeks after Will left, Amabel felt afraid all the time. She felt like she was being followed and that he might suddenly appear and try to hurt her. When she realised that this was not his style and that he would probably never contact her again she started to relax, but still felt very insecure. She felt ashamed and very sorry for herself and her family.

Amabel and her family had to pay around $4,000 in fines to the real estate company to break out of the contract for the apartment.

It would take Amabel a long time to trust anyone again. Each time she was presented with the opportunity to develop a relationship she would wonder if the person she was attracted to had bad intentions and what might go wrong. She and I remain friends and continue to stay in touch. Another stranger that I have never met, across the other side of the world, but one with whom I share a complete understanding of what we each went through.

◆　◆　◆

After July 2010 and Amabel, everything went silent and the flood of new victims stopped. I knew that either Will Jordan had changed his name to stop people finding out about his past or he was in jail again. However, it was inevitable that someday someone else would get in touch. It was only a matter of time.

The Hypnotist

Having had such success as the author of a memoir, I wanted to try my hand at writing a novel – currently still a work in progress, It involves regression hypnosis. It is a thriller involving regression hypnosis, so I started research into hypnotism as I needed to understand the process to include in the book. I contacted a couple of hypnotists to ask if I could interview them and also if they would hypnotise me and let me record it for research purposes. Of these, one encounter stood out.

When the hypnotist opened the door, there was a nice-looking chap with salt-and-pepper hair, good figure, average height. Just a normal bloke. But instantly our hands touched I felt a chemical attraction and it was obvious he felt it too. He had an intense look in his eyes and held my gaze intimately. I shook off the feeling, thinking how obvious I was making it that I was attracted to him – and got on with the interview. We talked about his background. He had initially been in the police force but had become disillusioned by the lack of positive change he was able to make in the community and how society seemed so dark. So he next went into a seminary and studied theology, becoming a minister for a while. However, he didn't feel that he was doing much good there so left and became a social worker instead. After years of doing that he had studied hypnotism and found he was passionate about how much it helped individuals overcome difficult issues and make real changes in their lives. Finally he had found where he belonged.

I was fascinated. All the while the man was talking he looked at me with those intense eyes. I was so drawn to him and instinctively felt a huge connection but at the same time mentally quite detached. This man was quite clearly a psychopath. I was even more fascinated because I could now see it so vividly. His focus on me was intoxicating. He talked about himself but it came across like he was trying to impress me. His body language was reflective of mine as he mirrored my movements, and he subtly complimented me on various things. He was starting to love-bomb me.

Knowing what I did now I could see what was going on. I could certainly feel the pull of this man but my understanding of how psychopaths work protected me like a shield.

We went through the hypnosis session, which I was recording (I don't think I would have gone ahead with it otherwise) but I didn't really go under all the way. I was too aware that I didn't want to give this chap free reign in my head. The session was very useful and gave me some good insight into hypnosis for my book. It also proved to me that I could now spot a psychopath. Truth be told, this wasn't too difficult as the three professions that toxic and controlling people get into are the police force, the clergy and social work because they are the professions that let them control other people easily. (Please note that I'm not suggesting all people in those professions are psychopaths though.)

Before I left, he told me (in quite a 'matter-of-fact' way) that it was clear to him that we would end up together but that I would need to decide when the time was right. I felt an extraordinary pull towards him, a massive instinctive attraction which intrigued me but, knowing what he was, allowed me to resist. I would not be seduced by him.

The next week I was going to the Edinburgh Book Festival. Jon Ronson was speaking about his book *The Psychopath Test* and had asked me to join him. So I invited the hypnotist to come along (as a thank you for allowing me to interview him). I knew my sisters were coming and wanted to know what they would make of him as well. I left a complimentary ticket for him on the door and he met up with us all in the bar after the event. My friends all thought he was very charming and were rather sweetly pleased that I had met someone who was obviously so interested in me.

My eldest sister, Lisa, took me aside and said, 'Don't touch him with a barge pole!'

I just grinned back and replied, 'I know. I just wanted to see if you would notice.'

As he took his leave later that evening, he looked intently into my eyes again and said, 'We are meant to be together, but I can see you are not ready yet, so get in touch when you are.'

I said goodbye and went back to have another drink with my sisters. I was never tempted to contact him, not even for a moment, and didn't think of him again until writing this!

I was very wary of men but being now able to spot the warning signs I felt a lot more confident about people. After a few years on my own, I had a brief relationship with one of my brother's closest friends – someone I had known for thirty years and so he was a safe bet.

He was lovely, and a fantastic kisser. He didn't like being permanently signed into technology so didn't check or answer his phone when he was with someone. And he was reliable. When he said he would do something, call me, or meet me, he did precisely that, and exactly on time. It was all so completely opposite to my relationship with Will Jordan. It was lovely for a couple of months. He liked that I was an international best-selling author and said he felt like he was dating a celebrity. However, although he was separated from his wife and living alone, he was still legally married, and felt guilty about having a relationship with someone else. Again, so different from Will Jordan. He didn't want to divorce because he didn't want to upset his children. So we split after just three months, but on cordial terms. I was sad but understood that children come first. It was nice that the last person to show me affection and intimacy was no longer Will Jordan and I felt that I had reclaimed my body from him, just like I had reclaimed my mind, my confidence, my finances and my emotions, step by careful step.

My children were still young. So I decided that I didn't need or want another relationship and that it was far better to be happy and alone than to introduce my children to another man who would disrupt our family. I made the conscious decision to remain single – certainly until the children were older.

Baptism of Fire

In 2010, although I was getting more confident in some areas I started to become less confident in others. I once more started to feel that I was living in fear. Will Jordan was no longer contained and was clearly victimising women again. When I was contacted by the new victims I would at least know roughly where he was and what he'd been doing, but contacts in the USA and Mexico had gone quiet. Will Jordan had disappeared and no more victims were coming forward. I knew he hadn't stopped but had just changed his name or done something to ensure his victims didn't find out who he was. Although he wasn't allowed back into the UK, I was still nervous that he might just find a way and it made me cautious. I felt that the walls of my life had shrunk inwards because of it.

In the late 1990s I had done a bungee jump – which is a whole other story in itself – and had learnt a very valuable lesson. When I stood on the platform above the stunning Cypriot sea, the man running the site said, 'When you are young, you are fearless. As you get older you build walls to protect yourself. You get bitten by a dog and start to fear dogs. You see someone get hit by a car and you get nervous crossing the road. You start to take the same route to work every day, talk to the same people, and watch the same TV programmes. You get into a rut – which is just a grave with the ends kicked out. Your comfort zone gets more and more restricted as there are fewer things you're comfortable with. Those walls make a box, and it gets smaller and smaller. You work, go home, watch TV and sleep, then get up and do it all over again, too scared to live or experience anything new. This bungee jump is so far outside your comfort zone that it will shatter the walls of your box forever. You will conquer fear itself. You have a choice now. You can let go and move forward, or you can step back into the box, continue to be afraid and face the consequences of inaction. If you do this . . . if you take this jump . . . you will shatter the walls of that box and be free!'

Without pausing, he then said he would count down from five and I would have to decide whether or not to jump.

He counted, '5, 4, 3, 2, 1!'

I dived into the air 150 feet above the crystal-clear ocean and screamed all the way down.

He was right though. It did shatter the walls of my world and opened me up to facing my fears instead of running from them.

So now, whenever I feel I'm getting fearful again I try to do something that will smash those walls down before they can build up again. In 2010, I decided I needed to do something drastic. I was becoming physically confident with the taekwondo but I was not emotionally confident. Then a friend told me about a fire-walking weekend in the north of England, and I decided to go along. It was another extraordinary experience. The man running it was rather larger than life and the first day was a huge build-up to the fire walk that night. There was a lot of motivational speaking and exercises to make us confident enough to overcome our fear and step out in our bare feet onto the red-hot burning coals.

The trouble was that the chap running the course seemed rather familiar to me. He told us he had been an intelligence officer and served for nineteen years in the SAS as a specialist trainer in interrogation techniques. He told the group about his experiences in Northern Ireland and Iraq and had indeed written a couple of books about his experiences as well. The group were spell-bound listening to him, each one of them hanging on his every word – but it just reminded me of the way Will Jordan would talk about his experiences and I simply didn't believe him. I told myself that it didn't matter and that he wasn't trying to get into our lives but only to fire us up enough that we could overcome our fears. I listened sceptically, which stopped me from becoming motivated, and so tried to gee myself up instead. We did various exercises and I managed to break a one-inch-thick piece of wood with the flat of my hand on the first try – my taekwondo training helped with that. Then it came time for us to build the fire.

We all helped to pile logs up and started the fire, and watched as it burned down and finally raked the red-hot embers into a circle about fifteen feet wide. Then we took our shoes and socks off and rolled our trousers up.

One by one my fellow attendees walked barefoot over the glowing red embers. I stood at the side and willed my feet to move but nothing happened. I was the last one left who had not done the walk – some of the others had now done it several times but I was still frozen to the spot. Finally two of my colleagues asked if they could do it with me, and side by side we took the walk. I only did it the once. It actually didn't hurt much because although they were burning hot embers my feet were only in contact with each point for a fraction of a second before moving on to the next step. It felt rather like walking barefoot over gravel, and I had a couple of hot-spot burns but nothing major. At least I had done it and that was liberating.

The next morning we all gathered for breakfast and the speaker sat opposite me, talking again about his work in the intelligence service. I asked him how he was recruited, and he looked surprised and then answered very vaguely while I listened and asked more specific questions. My friend who was with me and knew my story listened with interest. I then commented that it sounded very much like how my husband was recruited and my friend looked shocked. Suddenly my friend looked at the speaker in a new light. She had taken everything he had said at face value and believed that he was who he said he was. Now, as I started to question him, she started to see the holes in his story.

As we drove back to Edinburgh we talked about him and she was shocked that she'd been so taken in – she hadn't for a moment thought he might be lying. The point is that he could have been telling the truth about his career and experiences – after all, some people do do that kind of work, and they also talk about it once they are out of the service – but it's surprising how readily people are willing to believe a story, especially when they don't have a chance to question anything. It was interesting to watch the other eleven people in the group absorb what he was saying and believe him without question. This helped me understand slightly better how I myself had believed Will Jordan.

When I met the hypnotist I had felt the pull of attraction but managed to resist it. Now I seemed to be completely immune.

TOGETHERNESS

More fun things were happening with regards to my book and the opportunities it gave me. *The Bigamist* had been translated into Polish, Swedish, Czech and Flemish and was starting to sell internationally. Mainstream Publishing was taken over by Random House and my book took on a new lease of life as an e-book. (I had no idea how successful that was until I got an email from Jenny, my agent, stating the amount she had deposited in my account as my six-monthly royalties cheque for that period. I laughed and sent her a text saying she'd forgotten to include the decimal point. Then I had to sit down when she texted back with a smiley face saying that, no, she hadn't!)

I was offered a European tour, doing interviews, articles and radio shows in various different countries. Robyn still had separation anxiety though, and when I was setting off for the airport, she held me tightly and said, 'What if you don't come home? What if the plane crashes?' She was absolutely terrified of losing me. I would reassure her and call her at each stage of my journey to chat, and to let her know I was OK and that although out of sight she was never out of mind.

My friends Mandy and Carina were absolute godsends during this time. They would step in and help look after the children whenever I had to be away (and quite often when I just needed a break as well).

Robyn finally got over her separation anxiety when she went to school camp aged twelve. Having gone away somewhere herself I think she suddenly realised that I didn't just disappear. After that she was much more settled and less anxious for a while.

Robyn's father, Ross, didn't write to her or call her from Japan. He didn't even send her birthday or Christmas cards. He came back to Scotland in 2012 for a holiday, and announced it on Facebook to all his friends but didn't even contact me or his now thirteen-year-old daughter Robyn to arrange a visit. Robyn was 'friends' with him on Facebook so saw it all unfold. He finally got in contact – eight days into his two-week visit – to ask if he could see her. I tried to be supportive and asked Robyn what she wanted me to do about it. Did she want me to ignore it and just agree to a visit, or write to him saying what I thought of his behaviour? She said we should write. So I did. I told him that he would lose her if he didn't start showing her some interest. I said he had not supported her financially, physically or emotionally and was now being detrimental to her self-esteem by making her feel that she really didn't matter. I wanted to shock him into taking action, but it didn't work. Unsurprisingly, he responded aggressively by saying that he might be absent but I was far worse of a parent because I had let a paedophile into the house. He took the worst thing that had happened to me and tried to weaponise it against me.

I didn't reply to him, but I did write to his wife and his mother saying that I would not be talking to him ever again, and that if he wanted to discuss anything to do with Robyn he would have to do it through them. I have never spoken to him since.

Robyn met up with her father but shortly after that she decided to cut ties with Ross as well. It always had to be her decision and I'm glad she had the confidence to make it without having any negative emotions associated with it.

The children and I had such a good relationship. We were a loving and supportive family of four, plus Honey our dog. We had our spats (every family does) but usually we all got along and looked after each other. The media attention in my book had not waned and there were several documentary companies interested in filming with us. Each time the TV company would ask that the children speak to a psychologist beforehand to ensure there would be no fallback on them for any distress caused in the filming. Every time these calls were made, the psychologist would speak to them on the phone and then come back to me to tell me what they thought. To my delight, they were always surprised that my children were so stable and settled after their experience. In one case the psychologist said she had never come across children who were so 'together' and that we were clearly a very solid and secure family. It meant everything to me because it validated my philosophy of how to raise my young brood and meant that they were OK. No matter how strongly I felt about being honest and truthful and open with my children, it was good to be told by professionals that I had got it right.

DID HE EVER LOVE ME?

In 2012, I got a message from Dr Liane Leedom (author of *Just Like His Father?*, which I had read in 2006, and an expert in genetic connection to psychopathy and antisocial personality disorders). With two colleagues, Emily Geslien and Linda Hartoonian Almas, she was doing a study and wanted to use *The Bigamist* in a research report called *Did he ever love me? A qualitative study of life with a psychopathic husband*. I felt honoured and readily agreed.

The study was published in a journal, *Family & Intimate Partner Violence Quarterly*, in September 2012. I found it fascinating. It was the first in-depth study of the influence of psychopathy on the intimate behaviour of men. They used the published memoirs of ten women (including mine) who had been in long-term relationships with psychopathic men and analysed news articles, video interviews and author feedback to back them up. They did this against the backdrop of Dr Hare's PCL-R checklist. Interestingly, the report only looks at books written by women because they couldn't find any books written by men about their long-term relationships with a psychopathic wife. All of the victims in the study had been conned, manipulated or coerced during phases of their relationships and all of them had been exploited by their psychopathic partners.

They mentioned Dr Reid Meloy – another leading expert, and board-certified forensic psychologist and author, and a consultant on criminal and civil cases through the USA and Europe as well as for the FBI. In his book, *The Psychopathic Mind*, he suggested a continuum of scores to assess the PCL-R. He set a scale for those scoring 0 to 9 points being classed as 'non-psychopathic', those scoring 10 to 19 points as being 'mildly psychopathic', those scoring 20 to 29 points as being 'moderately psychopathic', and those scoring 30 to 40 points as being 'highly psychopathic'.

So even a score of 10 or above puts the participant on the psychopathic scale, and indeed we don't just have psychopaths and non-psychopaths but there is a whole sliding spectrum of psychopathic 'disturbance', as Dr Meloy calls it. All this means that when in a toxic relationship, rather than asking the question 'Is my partner a psychopath?', you should really ask the question 'How much psychopathic disturbance does my partner have?' It is estimated that around 1% of the general population is severely psychopathic but this figure may be misleading. Donna Anderson of LoveFraud estimates that around 10% of the general population would score 12 or more on the PCL-R and therefore fit into the diagnosis of psychopathy. That would mean that one in ten people are on the spectrum – a very frightening thought.

In Dr Leedom's report, *Did He Ever Love Me?*, the maximum score given to each of the other subjects researched was 36 – except in the case of Will Jordan. In that report, the psychologists involved unanimously gave him a maximum score, 40 out of 40 – giving my layman's diagnosis professional endorsement.

Dr Leedom's report also mentioned the connection for victims with Stockholm Syndrome. This term was coined in the 1973 case where bank robbers held a woman and three other people hostage in Stockholm for six days. When released, the female hostage found she had formed a strong attachment with her captor, and all the hostages defended their captors and wouldn't testify in court against them. There are four conditions involved in developing Stockholm Syndrome: a perceived threat to one's physical or psychological survival at the hands of the abuser(s); perceived small kindnesses from the abuser to the victim, and a feeling of dependency on them; isolation from perspectives other than those of the abuser; and perceived inescapability of the situation with little hope of outside intervention from family or friends.

Stockholm Syndrome (or traumatic bonding) can apply to any victim–perpetrator situation, including domestic abuse and child abuse where most of the above-mentioned conditions exist. When Stockholm Syndrome emerges, the victim can cling to the abuser because the victim perceives that this may be their only hope of survival. That unhealthy bond can be stronger than one that forms in healthy relationships. I experienced all four aspects of Stockholm Syndrome with Will Jordan. I felt under physical threat as he psychologically tortured and indoctrinated me into believing our lives were in danger, whilst also playing with my mothering instinct when he said that the children were most at risk from being kidnapped and ripped apart. Throughout our time together, he was showing me love and affection, as well as assuring me that he was the only person I could trust. I felt isolated because I believed that anyone I told would be put in danger as well, plus there was nothing anyone else could do to help me. All of this made my situation inescapable; there was no hope of help from outside. It all added up to make me completely dependent on Will Jordan. Towards the end of my relationship with him, when talking to social workers about his criminal past, I felt compelled to hold on to what Will Jordan had taught me – that he was the only person I could trust to keep our children safe.

Having read Dr Liane Leedom's book, I had the great pleasure of talking to her on Skype about raising the children of psychopaths. One of the warnings she gave me was that finding empathy and emotion in your children is good but you also have to look out for signs of self-regulation and impulse control – for instance that they show compromise. There is an inner triangle of traits that cover the ability to love, exercise impulse control and demonstrate moral reasoning. She said that by definition, a psychopath is someone with impairment in all three of these abilities.

'In the meantime,' she said, 'keep an eye out for substance abuse. Beware of them becoming addicted to drugs or alcohol – and be specifically aware if they show vandalism tendencies or the like.'

She explained to me that those at risk of psychopathy who also start substance abuse before the age of twenty-two are liable to end up as psychopathic (from alcohol abuse) or schizophrenic (from marijuana abuse, if used to excess).

Another point that Dr Leedom made was that we have a huge issue of tribal/family loyalty meaning that if someone is aware that a family member is psychopathic, they won't generally tell others about it. They will support the psychopathic adult child and sometimes even be relieved when a new victim of that psychopath is found because then the family will get some respite whilst the psychopath focuses on the new victim instead. It made me think about Will Jordan's parents again. Were they victims of his as well? Were they helping him because it meant he left them alone? Or were they instrumental in making him what he was, as well as benefitting from the money that he defrauded?

I felt like I had come so far. Not only did I now know and understand what Will Jordan was, but I was also learning so much more about psychopaths in general. My book was even being used by experts to further research the subject. But I still wanted to learn more. I wanted to understand the mechanisms that had allowed Will Jordan to control me. I now understood why he did what he did, but I wanted to know *how*.

I started digging deeper into the techniques that psychopaths use and came across a report by Dr Jeffrey Hancock and Dr Michael Woodworth called *Hungry like the wolf: A word-pattern analysis of the language of psychopaths*. It is fascinating, and I've included more detail about it in the Appendix, entitled 'Toxic Techniques'. Dr Woodworth said, 'You can spend two or three hours with a psychopath and come out feeling hypnotised.' Psychopaths are masters at distracting their victims; they tend to use body language and movement to distract and supplement their words. Their nonverbal behaviour is often so convincing and diverting that people don't recognise they are being deceitful. It reminded me rather like a snake moving its head to distract its prey. They are disturbingly good at manipulating people face to face, even with qualified research specialists, so although they express themselves verbally very clearly, their face-to-face and non-verbal communication is really the way they manipulate individuals.

Two of the techniques Hancock and Woodworth talked about in their report were incredibly familiar. They were called 'reframing' and 'nonsensical conversation'. Reframing – sometimes called 'projection' – is when someone turns any flaw or situation around to make it look like the other person is actually at fault. For instance, someone using projection might accuse their partner of being unfaithful when it is in fact the accuser that is having the affair. It is used to put the victim off balance and instil a sense of guilt even though the victim has done nothing wrong. I remember very clearly the situation when I was giving birth to my daughter and my son. My 'husband', instead of being by my side, managed to convince me he was in a locked-down war zone, struggling to survive. Although I was going through a dramatic and painful experience needing my partner by my side, I was made to feel guilty because I was led to believe that he was trapped, starving in a war zone and lucky to be alive. Indeed, he wasn't anywhere near a war zone and was just a few hundred miles down the road, busy wearing boots too small for him in order to persuade me eventually that he had been far, far away. He was absent both times when I was giving birth, and having me worry about him whilst going through that was the aim.

The other, and even more interesting technique I learnt about was 'nonsensical conversation' or 'word salad'. For example a psychopath will meander and continue talking with a confusing or unintelligible mixture of seemingly random words and phrases, roughly moving around the subject at hand but never really or not precisely coming to a point which will explain or excuse their behaviour, at least not initially, but 'there are reasons for that – something that will change everything . . .' This sentence, annoying and confusing as it is, is an example of word salad.

There are no reasons for it other than to keep the audience listening and becoming slightly hypnotised whilst awaiting some clarification.

It is deliberately never getting to the end of the sentence or the point they are making: psychopaths will continue talking until the victim finally interjects with a guess or suggestion of their own, giving the psychopath the very piece of information they need. When someone you care about is struggling to make a point, you naturally fill in the gaps, listening carefully to what they are saying and trying to make sense of it, sometimes even finishing their sentences and/or summarising what you 'think' they are trying to say as they meander on. 'Oh, I see, it's this . . .' The victim leaves this conversation with the only answer that fits, in their own head, with the person they believe their partner to be. They believe the conversation to have been resolved when in fact the psychopath has said nothing at all and left the victim to fill in the blanks, gaining information that will be key to attracting the victim and keeping them under control.

The extraordinary thing is that you don't notice it's happening until it's pointed out. However, now I knew I started to see it in people around me. I noticed it particularly in televised interviews of politicians with their avoidance of questions by using word salad and projection.

Suddenly I could see how Will Jordan had manipulated me, how he had used verbal techniques such as reframing and word salad, as well as conversation and emotional manipulation. He was a master of his art and I had given him the answers every time, the excuses that I would accept for being absent for births, Christmases and birthdays. I had told him my biggest fears – that of the children being taken away, abused and hurt. I had given him all the tools he needed to control me and manipulate me to do whatever he wanted.

I knew now though, and once that knowledge is there it cannot be taken away. I knew that no one would ever be able to control me like that again.

CAT AND MOUSE

In January 2014 Will Jordan re-emerged. I got an email from Mischele Lewis with a shocking tale of lies, deception, fraud and emotional trauma. She asked me to call her, so sitting cross-legged on the floor in front of my laptop, I dialled the international number and waited the long seconds for it to connect. The photographs on my computer screen were a harsh reminder of the pain I had gone through years ago. The face of my non-husband smiling out at me with his arms around another new victim.

The phone only rang a couple of times before it was answered by a gentle and slightly hesitant American accent. I knew exactly how she felt. I had answered a very similar call almost eight years earlier from my husband's other wife.

'Are you OK?' I asked Mischele. 'How are you feeling?'

'Angry!' she replied. 'I read your book overnight and I can't believe the similarities!'

Mischele told me the bones of her story. How she'd met Will Jordan online, how she had believed he was British and working for the Foreign and Commonwealth Office (FCO), flying drones and working in liaison with US intelligence.

Like me, she had been sucked in and had contact with others who validated his story. Like me, she was a single mother who'd been in an unhappy situation before meeting a man who seemed to be Mr Right.

Like me, she got engaged to him, lost money to him and then found out the truth.

'What will you do about the baby?' I asked, finding out she had recently become pregnant and aware that it was early enough in the relationship for her to have options.

'I don't know,' she said with genuine concern. 'I have to think about my existing children too.'

I understood entirely. There was a lot to consider and I am not sure what decision I would have made if I'd discovered the truth when only a few weeks pregnant.

Mischele was in shock, but unlike some of Will Jordan's victims she was not crushed. She was fired up. She reminded me of myself, someone with a burning desire to know more and understand what had happened. It was strange being on the other side of the phone call. To be the one knowing the truth and explaining to Mischele what he really was. Honestly though, I didn't have to say much because Mischele had already read my book and my whole story was there. It must have been so strange to her reading about my life with her fiancé, the father of her unborn child, the man she thought until just hours ago that she would spend the rest of her life with.

It felt good to help her though and I felt I had found a kindred spirit. A fighter who wasn't going to allow him to get away with it. A strong and fiery woman who would not be victimised nor feel embarrassed by what had happened. We talked for hours and she told me her story from the very beginning.

◆ ◆ ◆

In 2013 Mischele was a thirty-five-year-old labour and delivery nurse working in a maternity hospital in New Jersey, passionate about her job and mostly working nights which meant she had her days available for her two children. The first thing that struck me about her – seeing the photographs she sent me – was how stunningly beautiful she was, with long blonde hair and gorgeous big blue eyes.

In January 2013, Mischele was separated from her husband and in the process of divorce. She, like many others, decided to go online to look for love. She was not interested in 'playing the field' or shopping around. She just wanted to find a companion and partner for life.

She met forty-eight-year-old William Jordan, posing as forty-year-old Liam Allen, a British intelligence officer working for the FCO. Initially he told her that his name was Guillaume but that Americans found the name particularly hard to cope with, so he went by 'Liam'. He had recently returned to the USA and owned a medical records company. The conversation flowed easily and smoothly. He seemed to be everything that Mischele had ever wanted and they just 'clicked'. Liam came across as charming, intelligent, well read as well as being musically inclined.

As he got to know her, he spun her a story about how he was born in New Jersey but was sent to England as a toddler because his mother was abusive. His father had intervened after his mother had nearly put him in a scalding hot bath and he decided that Liam could no longer live with his parents, for his own safety. His father sent him to live with relatives who were Oxford University professors. Mischele felt very sorry for this poor man who had had such a sad life. Although his distant Oxford relatives provided for him, they were not particularly caring – they had other older children and treated him rather like a charity case.

Liam spoke with a British accent and explained that he had attended Oxford University before joining the British military and flying helicopters. He then admitted that because he was cunning and smart he had been offered a job with the UK Ministry of Defence doing a job where he was to go ahead of missions to befriend locals and persuade them to act as scouts for targeting high-ranking terrorists post 9/11. The scouts would then tell his team when the coast was clear and he would personally pilot the drones remotely in order to attack their intended target.

After Liam had left the military, he had taken his pension and gone to Mexico where he had fallen in love with a single mother who had a Down's Syndrome daughter. They were planning to get married and he wanted to take guardianship of the daughter, but then Hurricane Alex hit. After an arduous journey to the British Embassy in Mexico City he was flown back to New Jersey where his birth parents resided. Finally he was reconnecting with the parents who had sent him away. Liam had tried to arrange for his Mexican girlfriend to come to the USA but whilst he was in the process found out that she was cheating on him and ended the relationship. He was still paying for the daughter's schooling though. Liam even proudly showed Mischele a photograph of the daughter (who was in fact Amabel's little sister).

As with all the other women he had befriended, Will Jordan lied about his age, background, marital status, military background, parental status, income, education, job and even his name.

Mischele was love-bombed and seduced by this charming, attentive, lovely man who eventually after a couple of months opened up about his intelligence work. Liam sat her down to have a serious talk with her and told her about his 'real' job, working for the British government. He said he escorted embassy workers and foreign dignitaries, as well as their families, from place to place – he was a glorified bodyguard, sometimes flying helicopters and small airplanes in the line of duty.

Mischele had a lot of questions so she wrote them all down and they talked through them together, point by point.

Then in May 2013, Liam told Mischele that if they wanted to be together she would need to be vetted and get 'clearance', after which she'd get a secure phone to contact him on.

Mischele was duly contacted and asked to set up a 'digital voice fingerprint'. She had to call a specific number in Washington DC and say her name for voice-recognition software. The phone was answered with beeps and blips and then she had to say her name, then again, and then a third time. After being told that the fingerprint had been accepted she was then telephoned by a man calling himself 'Tom Chalmers'. Tom had a very English accent and initially talked to her in code about an 'Allen Tudor house' that she had shown interest in. Mischele was confused but pretty quickly realised it was code and carried on in the same vein. The 'Allen' house the man on the phone was talking about was actually Liam. Using this code, Tom discussed further details with Mischele on the phone and talked her through the vetting process. He then told her she would need to provide information and bank account details for her to be cleared, including making a payment of $1,300. This money would of course be returned to her. Mischele also had to fill out pages and pages of Official Secrets Act forms which would bind her to secrecy as well as give them all the information they needed for the vetting.

Mischele was then told there would be a series of tests. Tom said, 'At any given time, something could be untrue. It may be a test to see if we can depend on you.' It was vague and confusing and kept Mischele off balance. What could that 'something untrue' be? Mischele was not to trust anyone or anything – no matter who contacted her and no matter what she found out – because everything could be a test to see if she was trustworthy. Tom reiterated that it was important to check on and test Mischele and the details she provided so that Liam and his whole team would remain safe and uncompromised.

Like me, Mischele was privy to so-called secret information before it became public. This happened most notably in early June 2013 when they were going to a friend's wedding and Liam arrived saying that he had been helicoptered in because he was dealing with a major situation. A National Security Agency contractor had blown the whistle on the NSA's mass surveillance of US citizens. Before the evening was out, Liam was called back again into work as the fallout hit. Indeed, the news hit the public just days later of Edward Snowden's activities and his whistle-blowing on the NSA.

After all this, Mischele's security clearance application was handed to another operator called Marcus, who sounded a lot younger than Tom.

Marcus was more open and friendly with Mischele than Tom had been, and far more chatty. One day Marcus called her at 4 a.m. and let Mischele know the real reason Liam had left the British military years earlier. Marcus said that Liam had flown drones and his job was to kill terrorists. On one particular assignment, the targeted terrorist was among a group of innocent women and children, who would also have been killed by the drone strike. Liam's scout had recommended scrapping the mission but Liam's superior disagreed. Liam had refused the 'kill order' and instead flew the drone into a barn. Liam's superior was furious and called him undisciplined and unpatriotic. They even got into a physical fight over it. Both of them were discharged from the service with pensions that they'd accrued to that date.

Marcus and Tom were in contact with Mischele all through the summer, but in September 2013 their calls suddenly stopped even though the process wasn't complete.

Mischele was concerned but Liam gave her a quiet nudge and said, 'It could be a test to see how you react to being out of touch.'

Mischele felt overwhelmingly stressed by the whole process, not least because she was going through a divorce at the same time. She held it together though because above and beyond everything that was happening with Liam, she was a single working mother with children to look after and she had to stay strong for them.

By October 2013, Liam was talking about having a family together and was getting to know her mother, grandmother and children. The family pulled out all the stops to give Liam his first ever (as they had been led to believe) Thanksgiving dinner. At the same time Liam introduced Mischele to his newly reconnected parents. His father and mother both appeared delighted to meet her – neither said or did anything to refute the stories Liam had told her.

Shortly after that, Liam said he had never known what a 'soulmate' was until he had met Mischele. He said her family were wonderful and that he was falling in love with her children. On 8 December 2013, Liam proposed to Mischele and she accepted.

Liam didn't show up on Christmas Eve as promised, and on Christmas Day they waited for his imminent arrival. The children ran to the window, excited to be seeing him every time they heard a car drive past. Mischele and her family were disappointed as again he didn't show. Liam eventually arrived on New Year's Eve and spent the day with them but disappeared before the new year turned.

By January 2014 Mischele was growing very disenchanted with the relationship. She was debating ending things with Liam but then life threw her a curveball when she found out she was pregnant.

Liam had asked Mischele to have children with him and had talked about it for months, so she was confident that he would be delighted by the news. However, he wasn't. He distanced himself from her, saying that he needed time to 'process' the information. He left Mischele reeling at his reaction as he went to the bathroom. However, when he left the room he also left his wallet behind – something he'd never done before.

Mischele stared at the wallet for a while before deciding to look inside. Some instinct nagged at her that something was very wrong. She opened the wallet and found a bank card inside with the name 'William Allen Jordan' on it. Initially Mischele did nothing with this information. She shrugged it off as part of his work. After all, he had told her that he sometimes had to use false identities. For the baby's sake, Mischele tried to make the relationship work one last time, and the couple made plans to move in together and get married.

A few weeks later, after her fiancé and the father of her unborn child had stood her up on Valentine's Day, she decided to Google the name that she'd not managed to shake from her head. What she found made her physically sick. The first article was the story on Lovefraud.

com titled 'Will Allen Jordan, AKA Will Allen, convicted sex offender and bigamist, deported from the UK, returns to New Jersey'.

Mischele read that article and then several others. She saw reference to my book and downloaded it on her Kindle. She read it all in one night. In the morning she contacted me via my website.

That was when I called her: we talked for two hours.

Turning the Tables

The day after our first telephone call, Mischele confronted Will Jordan (as she now knew him to be called). Initially she didn't tell him that we had spoken but just that she'd seen articles about him.

Mischele thought that he would deny the articles were about him, or excuse them as lies, under-cover exercises or something like that. He didn't.

'I was a bastard,' he said. 'I did terrible things.'

He also said that he'd put all that behind him and wanted to be a better man. Meeting Mischele had changed everything for him.

Mischele listened to what he said, fully aware that it was all lies. She knew William Allen Jordan – this stranger who had wormed his way into her life – was a psychopath and as such was not interested in change. As a nurse she was also aware that psychopathy can be genetic and there was a chance her baby could also have the personality disorder. Someone with a strong maternal instinct, Mischele made the heart-breaking decision to terminate the pregnancy.

Overnight, Mischele's future – her fiancé, her new baby, her life – was wiped out and replaced by the knowledge that she had been in love with a paedophile psychopath.

Mischele and I talked and talked and kept in daily contact over those first traumatic days. I felt really connected to her as I knew exactly what she was going through.

Mischele let Will Jordan think that she was still in a relationship with him and was giving him an opening to build up the trust between them again. She let him think that he had a chance with her! Meanwhile, she considered what to do: an act of supreme control on her part.

I put Mischele in touch with six other victims, including his ex-wife from the UK and the recent victims from the USA. We created a private Facebook page so that we could all communicate and share stories. Mischele was stunned at the number of victims and keen to talk to each of them.

'It's like my story has a piece of everybody else's story in it,' she said.

'What do you want to do now?' I asked.

'He needs to be brought down!' she said. 'This needs to end with me!'

Mischele kept pretending to Will Jordan that she was willing to try again, but only if he worked to regain her trust.

Every time she spoke to him, she would talk to me immediately afterwards to ensure she kept grounded and also to share the information. In discussing what he said with me, it was easier to ascertain for her what was true, what was a lie and what was in between.

I had been working with a film company on making a documentary called *Evil Up Close* and we had just finished filming when Mischele got in touch. At the same time Mischele was talking to the police and finding out what they needed from her to make an arrest. Hard evidence was difficult to get because Will Jordan was an old hand at this and was good at not leaving a trail.

We talked to the film company and Mischele got hold of hidden cameras which they helped fit her with, a button camera on her shirt and another camera in her handbag. Armed with these, she told Will Jordan that they needed to talk and he needed to finally come clean about everything. She told him that she had now spoken to both me and his ex-wife from the UK and that she wanted to hear the whole story from his angle, including what was and wasn't true about the money she had paid for her 'security clearance'. He agreed.

Mischele drove to a Dunkin' Donuts café and after ordering a drink and a bagel, sat down to talk, all filmed on hidden cameras.

Mischele sent me the videos to watch and seeing Will Jordan again on camera was chilling and disturbing. Not least because, although a few years older and sporting a light beard and more scruffy clothes, he was exactly the same man I remembered. Mischele did an incredible job of appearing relaxed and open to his manipulations, talking casually with him initially as if absolutely nothing was wrong.

Looking at the footage, a lot of the conversation is difficult to hear because of the background noise, music and scraping of chairs in the café. However, some of it is crystal clear and quite unnerving. He uses so many different techniques when he talks. There's the engaging eye contact and open body language, and at first there is straightforward conversation. But whenever Mischele asks a difficult question there is also word salad, and nonsensical answers which distract Mischele from what she has asked. He says 'you know' and 'like' a lot throughout, and fills blank spaces with body language. This is a technique in itself, because if words are not used the victim will fill in the 'blank' body gestures with an answer that would fit. Usually, in being empathic and in trying to understand, we fall into the trap that prompts us to fill in the gaps and finish incomplete sentences for the person we love. Mischele mostly managed to avoid that but it is easy to see how it's done when you watch the video.

I transcribed the tape and it makes little sense when written down so I will paraphrase most of it here.

Mischele did an excellent undercover job of feigning vulnerability and interest in finding out his 'truth'. She turned the recording device on before she met him, psyching herself up to get him to talk.

Mischele: 'Turn it on before I get there, just in case he is early.

Hopefully by some grace of God he will confess everything.

OK, almost there, almost there, almost there.'

She sang along to 'Let it Go', which was playing on the car music system. She sang about never going back, letting go of the past and rising like the break of dawn. It was amazing how poignant the words were to this song – Mischele had previously told me that it had become her anthem during that time. She seemed to be singing it to steady her nerves, then she continued, talking to herself.

'One red light, one red light. Cheerio. Just breathe, just breathe. Be natural.

Just breathe, just breathe. Breathe. Breathe. Breathe in.

Normal. Normal. Normal. Be normal, be normal. Just "everyone want coffee?"

Oh, look at that, he's actually early . . . Bastard.'

She stopped the car and got out.

They walked into the Dunkin' Donuts café and ordered coffee and cinnamon raisin bagels, which Mischele paid for, then took their drinks and sat down. Will Jordan seemed particularly calm and not at all concerned or nervous about the conversation he was about to have. Mischele asked after his parents and Will responded that they were OK, and hopefully the change in the weather would make things better.

They moved through talking about various things until they started to discuss meeting up again the next day.

The conversation was evenly balanced, open, warm and relaxed. It flowed naturally. No one would have suspected that Will Jordan was about to spin a web of lies, nor that Mischele was secretly ensnaring him in a legal videotaped trap. About twenty minutes in, Mischele brought the conversation round to the subject at hand. She said: 'I don't know, I still have mixed feelings about everything.'

Almost immediately, the form of Will Jordan's conversation changed. Initially he used far more body language and shrugs, nods and hand gestures. Watching, I remembered what Dr Woodworth has said about spending time with a psychopath, that it is almost hypnotic and that a lot of the communication is through body language rather than individual words.

Will explained that it was completely understandable that she had mixed feelings and that he accepted that. That he could grovel but really he wanted her to see the bigger picture first, to know everything so he could then apologise for the right things because not everything he had told her was a lie.

He said that he could provide clarity but she would have to be in the right frame of mind, like when she was working at the hospital and having to tell people what was wrong with them and what wasn't, what they needed to do and when they needed to do it. It didn't matter what she said to those patients and how clearly she put it – if they were not in the right frame of mind they wouldn't see it. He said that similarly if she wasn't in the right frame of mind, no matter what he said she wouldn't believe him.

Will was already reframing the situation.

He then brought up the idea of the relationship not 'carrying forward' – that it wouldn't matter so much to him if he didn't care, that it would be easy to walk away if things were 'not balanced'.

Will was being deliberately vague and using unusually bland and vague terms for normal situations. This is done on purpose to keep the target focused on trying to understand what he is saying and distracting them from the point of the discussion.

Will admitted that he had already apologised for not telling Mischele the truth sooner and agreed that he should grovel about that, but that he didn't want to keep going over old ground. Mischele agreed.

Then Will started to explain, using word salad, that he hadn't done half the things he'd been accused of. That he was guilty of hurting people emotionally, yes, but that he'd been 'trollied' and set up. He wanted to break it all down into its basic parts so that Mischele could see the bigger picture and understand it all.

They then went on to discuss the situation between them and Will laid the groundwork of mistrust. He spent a good while talking about trust and knowing each other. He talked about being able to walk away, but then immediately stated that he had never done that. He had only ever stopped talking to someone and walked out of their lives after they had asked him to – he had never just disappeared. He had invested too much in Mischele to do that to her.

Mischele mentioned the paedophile conviction and that it was pretty hard for her to take – it was the last straw for her.

Initially, Will changed the subject to money. He said that his wife had had him over a barrel for twelve years after they were married and started to rant about how much money he had earned. That he had provided for his family and earned half a million, five times over, in the course of a year.

The distraction worked and Mischele moved on.

They then discussed the nanny who had committed suicide – the girl who had an affair with Will Jordan in the 1990s and, when rejected, had taken an overdose of paracetamol. Will talked about how he was there with her at the end and how she had been emotionally damaged by her own family. Her family were there at the end as well, and they blamed him, but he said that he just had to take that on the chin.

The conversation moved on to Will's wife in England, the woman who had contacted me on 5 April 2006 and been married to him when he targeted me. Will then told the story of how they had got together, how she was fun and although seven years older than him was still quite young when they met. She had been hurting and in the process of separating from her husband who was physically abusive. He said that she was pretty thin and 'very unremarkable' physically but a really nice person. She was weird and fun. He described her as 'very strong-willed, very loud-mouthed' and when she clashed with her ex it would end in a drag-out fight, something that Will said he could never have done. However, despite knowing this, he said, they had got together. She had liked his ability to make money, and he had liked her maternal side.

A lot of what this woman did had been about giving back to people in her life that she felt she owed. Again, that had fed Will's ego. They had bought her father a house, and a place for her aunt and uncle. They even took care of her mum. She had wanted him to make money and leave her alone to get on with her own life, and he had wanted the base and the challenge of getting out and 'chasing the dollar'. He even described it as 'better than sex sometimes'. It seemed like a good arrangement.

He explained that his wife in England liked the good life. She liked having the nannies, and to go travelling around the USA for a month – from one side of the country to another – and implied that she didn't really want him around. Will was OK with that, because it meant more time to himself. They were married but they lived very separate lives.

He talked about how he had had his 'partners' and she had 'played on the other side too', but within the midst of that was her religion. It had never left her and being in an open relationship like that didn't look good from the outside. Her family had got involved.

His wife had been fine with him having affairs as long as it wasn't in her face, but when his sister-in-law found out, she was furious and came after Will for cheating on her sibling.

Will Jordan continued to spin his tale to Mischele, saying that his sister-in-law had then fabricated evidence that Will had molested a girl under the age of thirteen and got him arrested. He said that his wife knew it was happening but realised too late that she had just ruined her meal ticket. Social services even ended up being suspicious because although his wife and her sister were calling him names to start with, Will's wife still wanted to take him back after his conviction.

Will made it all sound so plausible – that he was the victim of an elaborate charade – but declined to mention why he had pleaded guilty to the crime.

Will explained calmly and logically that the whole story was rubbish but that he had had to go through a whole three-year litany over it. He had been furious about having even been accused of molesting a minor. He would have left his wife at the time but it was cheaper to stay. He admitted that having affairs with the successive nannies was to some extent his bit of revenge for that.

He then explained how one nanny had had two children by him and he would have continued that relationship and run off with her, but then his wife had taken over and befriended the nanny so that she couldn't take him away, bringing her into the house to raise all the children together.

Mischele showed him a montage of photographs I had given her of ten of the children.

Mischele: 'I do have to say that you make beautiful small midgets.'

He just looked at it silently, not touching the iPad and then tapped the table with both hands.

Mischele: 'These two look like they could be twins. I can't pronounce her name.'

Will: 'Eilidh.'

Will just said that it was sad and that he couldn't connect with that, because what could he do?. How could he go there? After a bit more prodding by Mischele, he started to imply that he was more involved with the children than he let on. He said that leaving them was not a decision he had taken lightly, nor was it one he had made by himself. He hinted at writing and talking to someone in the UK and said that he knew everyone was OK. He said that he did 'things'. Most specifically, he stated outright that 'multiples of seven figures was left, for people to do whatever', clearly talking about money. He couldn't be part of the children's daily lives because that was not what other people would let him do and he didn't have the ability to argue with them. What's more, it would only have put them in an awkward position.

He hinted that he had sent birthday cards but that he suspected that the children never got them.

He feigned annoyance when Mischele asked about the abuse victim falling pregnant by him when she was twenty-one years old. This was something his ex-wife had told Mischele. With regards to the abuse victim, he said that she had left home at sixteen and got a Pakistani boyfriend. Will said that he was totally past it all now (meaning the sex offences conviction). That the abuse victim should have said, 'All right, stop, I don't wanna be a part of this.' Instead she had helped spread more poison. He implied that he had been set up when the girl and her mother asked to meet and talk somewhere, and when he arrived they accused him of something else (presumably getting her pregnant). He had provided for the children and provided millions of dollars in education and support. He implied that his ex-wife had manipulated and controlled him – that she could use other things against him but that didn't have the same effect as an accusation of paedophilia.

Will was talking in continually vague and confusing terms and not making a lot of sense. Mischele then moved on to talk about me.

Mischele: 'So where did Mary come into all this?'

Will went on to explain that he had set up an office in Edinburgh with six or seven people working for him. He and his wife had bought a big house up there and had three kids by that time. He had then met me and really fallen in love. He said:

> 'She was cute, she was incredible. She had a really good pep to her, she had good attitude. She was everything that [my wife] wasn't. More importantly, she wanted a future, she didn't just want [gestured money].'

So he was doing all kinds of different jobs and making money in order to separate from his wife.

Mischele asked if he had read my book, and initially he ignored the question. Later, however, he revealed more:

> Will: 'Well, I was also doing other jobs . . . And some of the things that Mary questions in her books – some of the jobs I was doing – like I said, not everything is a lie. Not everything is as far-fetched as it might seem. There was a lot of use that people have multiple passports . . . and chameleon wherever you have to adjust from. And quite honestly, at that stage . . . no real value about doing what needs to be done.'

It was word salad, but again hints that the CIA work was real and it revealed that he had indeed read my book. He described me as a 'kindred spirit' and also said there were things that he would just not be able to explain. However, he went into a detailed description of my life, almost all of it complete lies.

Will: 'Forget the book for a second, forget the perspective that's painted. You know how you have reacted to things like that. You know how you feel. And it is probably the same in this situation . . .

'Mary came from a very well-to-do family. She was the black sheep. Her family were very respected in Edinburgh, her father was a VP at the BBC and her mum was actually Scottish royalty . . .

'Scottish royalty doesn't mean much because they are part of the UK now, but at some point in time it would have meant something. And up there it still does mean something because they are a very nationalistic type of people . . .

'So for her that was a big deal, that was a really big deal. Um, and her mum was lovely, I liked her parents, but I loved her mum – I wished she was mine – she was an amazing, amazing woman. She was very much that kind of dour . . . you know that something just has to be done, this is the way it is . . . She was just this really good host.

'Mary was a nonconformist; her first move was to go rush out and drop out of school. Hooked up with this guy who played guitar; he sang in a bitsy band and had a kid within five seconds of whoever he happened to be with. She was a groupie. Had a little kid by him. And she lived in a little flat. But she was on, I think, her 3rd mortgage. [laughs]

'She had a relationship with her parents, her cousins, her child . . . [several hand motions] and she worked for Midlothian Council, so she was probably on about 20 or 30 grand a year – which for Edinburgh is not that much.

'She was very quick: she could put A, plus B, plus C, plus D, "that means if I do this, this and this", then she can apply logic to it.

'So after we first got together . . . at first I thought I wouldn't tell her anything, but she could see where things were going.

'I mean I was happy; I was genuinely happy. That was the greatest loss of that whole era [circular hands] for me, because she was an amazing person.

'She reasoned, if you are happy to play along, then I am happy with this. You don't have to live here; you don't have to do what you are doing. If you want to start up a business – because she had always wanted to start up her own business. You have got your reasons – do it!

'I get in this car that doesn't start every couple of days. She said, "All right, let's get you a car, let's build a life here! You're going to have to pay X amount of money into this bank account." And she walked the walk. Again, as long as it was not something that was in her face. It wouldn't

131

be up there, that was the whole point. We would never criss-cross each other. Before we got happy, it's just – I call it God's will of the mongrels that we came here, because OK, enough is enough . . . um, but that was fine – that went on for years – we were together for five years, I think.'

Mischele: 'Five or six years, I think she said.'

Will: 'And that, you know, quite honestly, that would have gone on forever. It wouldn't have changed.'

Mischele: 'Wouldn't it have been easier to leave [your wife] and then you could've just lived happily ever after with Mary?'

Will: 'And that was kind of where things were getting to . . . We had a separate company up there. Money was being funnelled into things . . . It was being funnelled into the house in her name. I trusted her. It's not like I had an "us" thing. I trusted her. OK, fine, the house needs to be in her name, the bank account needs to be in her name – so on and so forth. So that these things won't cause an issue all of a sudden, "Well, I want [hand chop motion] to get everything". . . . Keep in mind . . . All I was interested in was making sure that, OK, you guys can still carry on living – and I wanna do the same. I didn't go through all this and work this hard to wind up trying to find change for a coffee. Yeah, I was manipulating and manoeuvring things so that I could break and move somewhere else.'

He then went on to say that I was complicit in his plan. That what hurt him the most about my book was that I had denied I'd been involved in his plan all along. But then he also said that he got it. He understood that I had to 'wave a flag' to ensure people didn't think I was involved in his deceptions and had in fact been left lots of money, 'multiples of seven figures' as he said before. (I do remember getting phone calls from the other wife asking if I had got money from him, I assume now because he was telling her the same thing. At the time I was distracted by having found out my mother was terminally ill.)

Will: 'And yeah, [my wife] is nothing if not efficient. She's like a dog with a bone when she starts something [makes scratching hand action on the table with his fingers]. Start thinking, "OK, you have a job. Where is all the money? [drumming fingers on table] . . . Where's the rest of the money?" But – she's waving that flag, and all that just gets swept under the carpet. And I felt, truthfully, I felt outfoxed. I couldn't see that coming. Couldn't see that coming. Because there was nothing I had stuffed under a mattress, for me personally. I hadn't done that. Because it had never crossed my mind. What was under the mattress for me was in that scenario. I had never thought about that – so I thought kinda like, "OK. Learnt your lesson."

'And . . . you know – that's the mess of this – really – underneath all that. It's always expensive . . .

'And . . . both of them, despite anything I might say about them, have been the best they can in their own way, given their situation. The money left them, I am assuming it has gone on all the things that it should have gone on. Certainly from [my wife]'s perspective, if nothing, she has always taken excellent care of the children, that is a big thing for her.'

Mischele: 'She says she is on government assistance now.'

Will: 'It's not the same as it is here . . . She is not on welfare. Over there, as a mother with children, you get a certain amount of assistance no matter what. And it doesn't go to the men, it goes directly to the children. Because they had so much trouble with the men drinking and all that. So it is literally for the children. So let's just say that she is a master of not, not getting what she should get. How she fares specifically, who knows, how much she makes, whether she is with somebody else [shrugs], I don't know.'

Mischele: 'Neither one of them have moved on since.'

Will: 'Well, they've both kind of done [waves his hand back and forth], but like I said, I am not a fountain of information.'

(All the stuff Will Jordan said about me was nonsense. Ridiculously though, the thing that annoyed me the most wasn't his outrageous accusation that not only was I complicit in his plan and married him knowing he was already married with children, nor that I had 'multiples of seven figures' of his money and owned at least one house that he had paid for. The thing that irritated me was his saying that I was the 'black sheep' of the family, having dropped out of school with no qualifications, become a 'groupie' and got pregnant from sleeping around. Especially as I am a learning junkie and have two degrees and several business diplomas to my name – my first degree being in music. I wasn't a 'groupie', I was one of the musicians!)

After that, Will started to talk about being able to disappear, having contacts and preparing to step into a new life if he needed to. He talked in practical terms about what you needed to do to achieve that.

Mischele asked about the other American victims, and what had happened when he disappeared for four years (from July 2010 to 2014). He just said he was on his own, four years without sex, so that he could change his name and social security number, change his identity and disappear from scrutiny. But then he had met Mischele and they had just clicked.

> He said: 'Because – it's a click! [Hands outstretched] Like . . . no different than when I talk about Mary. I wasn't looking. That's what she turned out to be. There were Marys before, there were none after her. I wasn't looking for that, I didn't expect that. And I don't think life just completely gives you what you want when you just wait for it. I think sometimes . . . You know, you're a very special person. And if you look at us, it was very difficult actually trying to be clear with that because I genuinely had to deal with a karma check. Because you had things you were going through, and I – and I really had to do that kind of karma check.'

They briefly talked about Mischele's divorce and then Mischele brought the subject back round.

> Mischele: 'Like I said, I have a lot of "whys" more than anything. And I appreciate hearing your side of the story, like you have no idea how much I appreciate all this. I do, I really, really do, because, like I said, I'm trying to find my own course in this whole thing.'

> Will: 'And I'm purposely trying to – really a good picture – a good – as bad a picture as – I was bad – to deny that

means to deny who I am. Because you can't appreciate this if you don't know the past.'

Mischele: 'Because like, I'm still trying to figure out who you are. Who we are.'

Will: 'I'm the same person as when you met me. We are the same couple that we were. And . . . I know it's gonna sound condescending and it's really not meant to be, it's true. If you really were very lucky in life, you will never have to walk in the shoes that put you in the position where you have to do things. Because when you live life the right way, do things the right way, treat people the way you should treat them . . . you don't wind up in places where you're forced to do that. That's the truth. That's the God's honest truth.

'We can't get this time back, it's gone.'

Mischele: 'And that's exactly how I feel, it's like . . . because like, I feel like I have – my perspective is like I feel like I have been amazing to you in the last year, and I feel like you shit on me.'

Will: 'And that would be inappropriate, especially given what you have . . .'

Mischele: 'And it feels yucky. Honestly, so look . . . it really has taken a lot to not just go "fuck you", punch you in the face and walk away. Because trust me, I've thought about it. But it's like . . .'

Will: 'And I would've expected it, dealt with it, and then . . . at the end of the day, no one could fault you for . . .'

Mischele: 'Because it's like, the last couple of months it's been very difficult!'

Will started asking about the time, but the tape is muffled and I can't work out exactly what he was saying.

Mischele: 'I have no idea. Uhh . . . [picks up phone to check time] Two.'

Will: 'OK . . . uh, I need to go. But I get it, you don't have to blame others for the past. That's your bit of – and having to decide what's important, how it's important.'

Mischele: 'And like I said, that's why I want to . . . hear you out before I come up with a final conclusion. Because I feel like I owe myself that. Because I – that whole thing with my ex, I feel like I shoved it through . . . superfast. And then I introduced you into the lives of my kids, my mom, my grandmother, my colleagues . . . and completely incorporated you, and didn't even get half of that in return. Because you always kept me at a distance, and you like . . . denied me the communication and stability that I begged and begged and begged you for.'

Will: 'Which again, I feel that – at the time, I thought I had to do. And explained why. And even if you don't agree, at least you've got perspective to understand from now.

And you can forget it that way. In terms of your family, in terms of the kids, things like that – yeah.'

Mischele: 'I'm trying to be patient, but I feel like I've been patient for a very long time. And I know it's coming – it's coming.'

Will: 'No no, not even about it coming. At some point in time, even fearing psychologically . . . you have to have your little [draws line on desk] line in the sand. And you've got to – hmmm . . . I don't know what it is, I don't need to know. Point is, as far as you know between doing this and this, I'll be honest with you about how I can do it and when I can do it. And I'm not pulling punches. It's a different kind of conversation. It's a different kind of reveal. [noise] I haven't been pulling punches, I haven't flinched away, or broken eye contact and changed the subject. I've tried to be as solid as I can about some of the more difficult subjects [chopping table].'

Mischele: 'And like I've said, I appreciated your candour.'

Will: 'At the end of the day, if you've reached that point where OK, it's not fast enough or it's not worth it, then OK, and it's not worth it. It is what it is. At least it won't be because the effort wasn't made to actually do something, it'll be because of any other number of things that you, just being that kind of person that you are – would've had to carry forward – doubts and self-doubts or any kind of . . .'

Mischele: 'I have a lot of that.'

Will: 'You don't deserve that. And in all this time, if it's served no other purpose than to put those in perspective, then it's worth it. Because I don't want to spend the rest of my life not talking to anybody . . . having life in divorce. And if you tried to leave, I'd try to leave that . . .

'I've got enough of that crud I carry; I'm not trying to make any more of it. I think it could be something – but I'm perfectly prepared to – if that's the case – at least you're in a place . . . So that's how . . . I justify those to myself. And that makes it work.'

Mischele: 'Just waiting for some more clarity.'

Will: 'It's coming. Hopefully it's a little more clear now than it was at 11 . . . and then we'll just [chops across table].'

Mischele: 'It is. And like I said, I do . . .'

Will: 'Should we do this in your car? I've got some meetings.'

They picked up their stuff and got into the car to drive away. In the car, Will asked Mischele to drop him somewhere she had not been before. They talked about general stuff again, and then Mischele said:

'I don't know, sometimes I just wonder, why me? I have the shittiest luck in life. That's why you coming along was so amazing because it was going to be different. It was going to be a fresh start. It was going to be amazing.'

Will: 'It still is amazing. It was amazing and you're amazing.'

Mischele: 'But you have to make it a fresh start.'

Will: 'Mmm mmm [yes].'

Mischele: 'I know you are trying and I'm . . . seriously trying to be patient, I really am.'

Will: 'We do the very best we can with what we have to work with. Hopefully that coincides with you doing the same. That's all I can ask. I can't do any better than that.'

Mischele: 'I'm trying.'

Will: 'And me. Grand expectations and all – something that never happens.'

Mischele: 'I make no guarantees but I am trying to be fair and open and honest.'

Will: 'That's all I can ask of you. That is all you are asking of me.'

Mischele: 'Exactly. Especially like that HONESTY part. It's killing me.'

Will: 'Just here – drop me just here.'

They said their goodbyes and Will got out the car and walked away. As Mischele drove off, she spoke to herself and the people who would watch the video.

> Mischele: 'It's all bullshit, bullshit, bullshit, bullshit – that's all it is. Just bullshit and lies. Plaza 14/15, route 70. That's where we dropped him off. Does he live here? Does he work here? What does he do? Fuck knows!
>
> 'Jesus, God help me,' she said, with a deep sigh.
>
> 'If I can get this in tomorrow, if I can get the other footage with the confession with everything, you blow it. We'll see.
>
> 'Jesus, Mary and Joseph.
>
> 'I'm not even Catholic!'

◆ ◆ ◆

I found transcribing the video utterly fascinating and, equally, extremely unnerving. It allowed me to analyse Will's body language and word structure in detail, and really very little of it makes sense written down. It truly is the body language that matters so much.

Will Jordan explained away his dealings one by one in a completely reasonable tone of voice, as if he was actually the injured party but still being magnanimous about it all. He left gaps in his explanations and used gestures which made Mischele finish the sentence.

The utterly strange thing about listening to him talk on the video is that I had to keep slapping myself mentally, because I started to think 'Does he really think this?' and had to remind myself that he really doesn't. He knows exactly what he is doing and his tactics are very clear.

He uses projection and reframing – making it seem like his crimes against others, conning them out of money and manipulating them, were actually committed against him. He uses word salad and non-sensical conversation when Mischele asks a question, giving long and unintelligible answers which distract her whilst yet not answering the questions. And he tries to play on her emotions by stating how much he loved me, and how that was the 'biggest regret from that time' – I assume to try and make her jealous (and/or desire to be loved by him like that as well). That is all that is.

When Mischele asked him about the conviction for sexual offences against a young girl, Will shrugged it off as his wife's revenge for his affairs – even though he pleaded guilty to that in court and was given a fifteen-month prison sentence for it. He explained to another victim that he had pleaded guilty purely to protect the girl from having to testify at trial, something he now realised was a mistake because that conviction follows him around.

Although Will Jordan didn't admit to his crimes in this particular three-hour conversation, Mischele was not going to give up.

END GAME

In a supreme act of control, Mischele continued to string Will Jordan along day by day, gathering more and more information. She had hours of video footage including conversations with his parents who seemed (just like Will Jordan himself) to be totally relaxed and friendly around her.

Weeks went by and she was getting more distressed and nervous. Mischele's mother talked to me, worried about her daughter. Not just with regard to her mental state but in case she was in real physical danger from Will.

Then one day I got a frantic message from Mischele's mother. Mischele had gone missing.

Half a day had gone by and there was no sign of Mischele. Her mum had already called the police and because of the situation (and the fact they had been working with Mischele to assist her in gathering evidence), they ignored the 'has to be missing for twenty-four hours' rule and were already looking for her.

I tried to reassure Mischele's mother that I didn't think Will Jordan was violent or physically dangerous. However, I was reminded of an account from one of the British victims of how he had exploded in rage and held her against the wall by the throat – all because she had challenged him. I had never seen Will Jordan angry, and only ever once experienced his ire over the phone (after I answered police questions about my car being driven by my 'husband', thereby highlighting to them that he was actually a bigamist).

I was worried about Mischele, and her mother was terrified. We called and called Mischele's phone and sent messages via email and Messenger, just hoping something simple had taken her away and offline.

Finally Mischele reappeared. She had retreated into herself due to the emotional stress and decided to take herself off, away from everything for the day. She had gone down to the beach and walked and walked for hours (having switched her phone off and left it in the car). When she returned, she was embarrassed to see so many calls and messages. We were just so glad that she was OK.

Then eventually, after ten weeks of playing a cat and mouse game of psychological chess with a psychopath, Mischele had the evidence she needed. Will Jordan had confessed on camera to conning her out of the money she paid for her 'security clearance' with Tom Chalmers.

In April 2014, working with the police, she contacted Will to arrange to meet in the parking lot of a local shopping mall. Mischele watched as he arrived and was put in handcuffs and was ushered into the back of a police vehicle.

William Allen Jordan was charged with fraud and 'rape by deception'. What is more, Mischele told me that US Homeland Security were investigating him as he had been claiming to be a foreign spy on American soil!

Mischele could finally relax a little.

◆ ◆ ◆

Like me, Mischele decided she had nothing to be ashamed or embarrassed about and so went public with her story. It came out in the local papers five months later, in September 2014, shortly after Will Jordan was bailed out of jail by his parents.

A few weeks after that, another woman got in touch with Mischele and me. She had seen the photo of her new boyfriend in the papers and decided to make contact. This woman had known Will's father, John, from the local bowling club for the past five years. One day John had brought Will into the club and introduced him to her. They had clicked right away and started dating – until she saw the newspaper article about his arrest and what he had done to Mischele. The woman was astonished that Will's father, a man she had known for several years, had thrown her to his son with no concern for her welfare!

Will Jordan was brought to trial on 6 February 2015 and pleaded guilty to fraud. The charge of rape by deception was dropped as it was too difficult to prove, and he had been offered and accepted a three-year plea deal for admitting his guilt to fraud. The Homeland Security investigation wasn't pursued – presumably when they realised he was not a foreign spy they didn't think it worth taking further. Mischele was incensed that he was getting away with the personal harm he had done and was only being held accountable for the financial fraud, but there was nothing more she could do. An incredibly strong woman, she was undeterred and heroically set about changing the law in the USA to make 'sexual assault by deception' easier to prosecute. That in itself is a different story!

Mischele and I continued to talk regularly then and we still do. She is a formidable and powerful woman who felt just as strongly as I still do about stopping Will Jordan, or at the very least slowing him down. We both felt it really important to do everything we could to protect future victims.

Together we appeared on various TV shows in the USA and UK, shows like *The Security Brief* and *NBC Dateline*, as well as making numerous documentaries such as *The Internet Date from Hell*, *Evil Up Close* and *Handsome Devils*.

After each show we were contacted by new victims, each with their own story to tell, but always with the same theme: love-bombing, lies, deception, gaslighting and fraud. Will Jordan repeats his pattern over and over again. The only way to show or prove that is to make those stories public, to tell them over and over again. However, I am sure that my readers understand the pattern by now. Each and every time, when caught, Will Jordan says that he wants to change and that 'finally' he has found his 'soulmate' and of course he won't do the same to the next woman.

One story really hit me though, and demonstrated a darker side to Will Jordan's actions. A woman called Belle contacted us after our *NBC Dateline* episode. Extraordinarily, she had sat down on the remote control whilst changing her clothes for work, and the channel had changed to NBC. There on the screen was the man who had disappeared from her life two years earlier with no explanation or comment. She thought he had committed suicide.

BELLE

Around about the same time as Mischele was starting to get to know Will Jordan in February 2012, Belle was thirty-one and living in Philadelphia. It was then that Belle met Guillaume Jones-Jordan, a thirty-seven-year-old paediatrician from New Jersey.

Belle had already had a challenging life. Her father died when her mother was eight months pregnant with her and then her mother died of stomach cancer when she was still young. Orphaned at such a tender age, she was sent away to her mother's best friend in Australia and shipped off across the world to a whole new life. As if this wasn't enough to deal with, Belle was also a victim of abuse at the hands of the man she thought of as her grandfather.

At sixteen she came back to the USA and sought emancipation (emancipation of minors is a legal mechanism in the USA by which a child before attaining the age of majority is freed from control by their parents or guardians, and the parents or guardians are freed from any and all responsibility toward the child) so that she could live by herself without a legal guardian. She fell in love with her high-school sweetheart and married him whilst still only sixteen years old. She had twins when she was seventeen, a daughter at eighteen years old, and then her fourth child in 2002 when she was twenty-one.

Belle was a stay-at-home mum but when the children started school she put herself through college and became a nurse. She told me that her marriage was not a happy one though. Her husband was verbally abusive and then became violent. When he finally got another woman pregnant, Belle filed for divorce and by the time she was thirty-one had been single for a year and was feeling a bit lonely.

Belle tried to keep busy but was persuaded by her friends to go online to find 'love'. She went onto Craigslist to see what was out there. A picture came up of a decent-looking guy wearing hospital scrubs and stating his name was Guillaume Jones-Jordan. He seemed to have a good job and came across as a nice normal man. Feeling she had something in common with this chap because he too worked in a hospital, she messaged him.

They messaged back and forth for three weeks and he seemed really genuine. They talked on the phone and via text, every day and all day. Belle found Guillaume's name difficult to say so he told her to 'just call me Gee'.

Finally they decided to meet and arranged to have coffee. Belle's cousin lived with her and the children so she didn't have to worry about childcare arrangements. Her children were now fourteen, thirteen and ten so she was able to have some freedom, as long as she was back in time to get them up in the morning.

On the day they met in person, Gee drove from New Jersey to Philadelphia to pick her up and they went to a café. Things just seemed to flow so naturally. They talked for hours and he shared his background with her. He told her how his dad worked and his mother was bipolar, and when he was a toddler she had punished him in bad ways. Once she had plunged him into boiling water scalding his groin – he still had the burn scars all around his groin and upper thighs. Another time she had put him outside in the snow with just a shirt and a nappy on and a neighbour had found him and reported it to his father. His father had been so worried that he had sent Gee to England to live with relatives there in Oxford. Belle asked him why he had never got skin grafts for the burns and he answered that his father had just wanted to get him away and safe to England, so the scars just healed on their own.

Gee said that Oxford was OK and he liked it, but the other kids in the household didn't like him. It made him study more and he received a good education, getting his medical degree and specialising in paediatric trauma. He had had relationships – in fact he had married young with an older woman who didn't tell him she was infertile and couldn't have children. When that marriage failed, he travelled a lot and did internships at different hospitals. He spent a year working for SMILE, the charity that provides operations for disadvantaged children. He had had a relationship with a girl in Mexico but when he moved back to the USA, she didn't want to come with him nor continue the relationship long distance, so that had ended too. He had had another relationship with a girl in Texas but she was 'crazy' and so he had ended that. As for work, although he was a medical doctor and a surgeon, Gee's degree and qualifications were from the UK and not the USA so he had to work at the hospital as a 'nurse practitioner' until he had completed 200 hours of service and passed an assessment.

Belle bonded with Gee, having a similar background. She knew what it was like to lose family and be sent away overseas. She recognised this 'damaged' man as someone similar to herself, someone who had risen above the difficulties put in his way.

They were getting along so well over coffee that Gee said he would take her to his favourite restaurant for something to eat – just over the state line in New Jersey. They set off in his car, but the 'favourite place' was closed. He said he knew a hotel nearby with a bar.

Belle said, 'No, I am not going to a hotel,' but Gee reassured her that they were just going there for a drink and nothing else, so she agreed. He seemed so gentlemanly and safe that she didn't think too much of it.

In the bar, Belle had a couple of glasses of wine. There was no food so the wine made her feel a bit woozy. The next thing she was aware of was waking up in a hotel room naked beside Gee. She was disorientated and confused but he told her that she'd passed out, having got drunk in the bar, and so he had felt it was not prudent to take her home, but had instead got a hotel room for them both. She felt deeply embarrassed that she had got so drunk so quickly, but then she'd not had anything to eat so it was certainly understandable. The one thing that was clear was that Gee was still being a gentleman and showing concern for her well-being. Belle apologised for getting so inebriated.

He drove her home before morning so that she would be back before her children woke up.

Three days later they met up again. He brought her flowers and they went out for a nice meal together. They met again about two to three days every week after that. He seemed to have a lot of money and bought her presents, taking her out and looking after her. She met up with him at the children's hospital where he worked, St Christopher's. He met her in his scrubs with the hospital logo on them and seemed perfectly at ease in his workplace. Often she would see him with large amounts of cash, thousands of dollars in a book bag. She queried why he had so much cash and he told her that it was a hangover from living in England where people were less trusting of banks. He said he was changing bank accounts and so had taken his salary out in cash to put into another bank. Belle was pretty worldly-wise and told him that was nonsense, but he just said he was saving up and had a surprise for her but that she would have to wait to find out what.

On their third date, Gee said that he was exhausted so could they just get a pizza and go back to his apartment and watch a movie instead. That was the first time she saw where he lived – an apartment just off the Kings Highway in Cherry Hill, New Jersey. It was a pleasant enough one-bedroom apartment with a kitchen, living room, bathroom and bedroom. There was space for a desk and Belle noticed the medical patient files on his desk – Gee said that he needed the office space when he worked at home. She also saw bills and credit cards in the name of

Guillaume Jones-Jordan on his desk. After some time, Gee gave her a key to the apartment and the code to the main entrance and they stayed there together about four nights a week. Because of her previous experience with her husband, Belle decided not to introduce him to her children, at least not yet, and so she was always home before morning.

When their relationship turned intimate Belle saw the burn scars around his groin. They were visible and quite noticeable. Gee said that the scars put some women off and that he was embarrassed by them. She reassured him that she didn't find them a problem.

One day Gee told her that he had a confession about the money. He had been saving up to buy a house and do it up for him and her and her children to be together. He wanted them to live in a decent area so the kids could go to a good school and would be picked up each morning by the school bus that went past.

He took her to see the house. It was beautiful. He had the key already and took her inside to view the unfinished 'work in progress'. His tools were in the kitchen and he had clearly been working on doing the place up. He lit a fire and they made a makeshift bed and stayed there all night making plans for their future. Gee told her he wanted them to have a child together and when Belle commented that she needed to go out to get more birth control he begged her not to.

Then things started to change. Gee's mother went into hospital and he fell on hard times trying to support his parents and her medical bills. Belle never met his father but spoke to him on the phone a few times and Gee referred to her as his father's 'future daughter-in-law'. Gee's father called him one day and Belle could tell from the phone call that he was asking Gee for money again. His father didn't have enough to pay for his mother's medication and Gee said he had no more to give. Belle offered to help out financially – she told Gee to tell his father that they would sort it and proceeded to give Gee $50 to $100 at a time. After all, she was seeing this relationship as a long-term thing and so was contributing to the family that she was becoming part of. Plus Gee would soon be getting a much better salary once he had completed his 200 hours working in an American hospital and got his licence to practise surgery there.

Sometimes Gee had to go on trips, medical conferences and the like, usually only for a few days here and there. Once he went back to England and said that he wanted to take Belle with him but knew she would not be able to leave the kids for that long.

One time, Belle remembers they were stopped by the police. Belle was stunned at how smooth Gee was with them, very calm and professional. Gee explained that he was driving his father's car and so didn't have the papers. He made a show of looking for his driving licence but couldn't find it. The policeman simply let him off with no warning or citation. Belle asked him how he knew the way to talk to the police so confidently and he explained that he had had some dealings with the police force in a professional capacity in England and knew what to say because of that.

In July 2012 Belle got sick one evening while having dinner at his apartment. Gee excitedly suggested that she might be pregnant. Belle didn't think this was possible and replied, 'Slim chance!' He insisted that he run across the road for a pregnancy test. It was positive. Gee was very excited and Belle was stunned.

Gee phoned his father to tell him and then passed the phone to Belle. His father congratulated her and said, 'Our first grandchild! This is going to help Gee's mum so much; it's going to give her something to look forward to and fight for.' Gee and his father's excitement started to rub off on Belle and she started to be excited as well. Gee wanted to finally meet her other children and Belle said she would consider it, but not yet. Her past relationship was holding her back from exposing her children to another man until everything was completely secure.

After Belle got pregnant, Gee told her not to come to the house he was doing up for them any more. He delightedly told her that he was building an extra room onto the bedroom as a nursery and therefore had got more workmen in. There was dust everywhere which wouldn't be good for her or the baby. Belle didn't see that as a problem but mostly stayed away until one day when she just popped down to see how it was all going. When there, she noticed some children's shoes and clothing as well as some women's items in the house. She pulled Gee up about it and asked what was going on. He told her that he had been clearing out the cupboards and found trash left behind and was just throwing it all away. He even showed her around the back of the house where there were lots of trash bags and berated her for not trusting him.

Then in September 2012 Belle had a miscarriage. Gee said it was her fault and that he blamed her, saying he was heartbroken. He appeared to become depressed, and they only saw each other once or twice a week. When they did see each other, Gee wanted emotional support. He asked Belle to let him nurse and suckle from her breasts, making the milk come in. She allowed it because it made him happy and would simply watch her shows and have a snack whilst he laid beside her with his head in her chest. Afterwards, he would be turned on and they would have sex. Gee said he had issues due to his mother's abuse and one of the things he found so attractive about Belle was her maternal instinct. This went on for months until finally Gee seemed to be in a better place and wanted them to try again for a baby.

For a few weeks Gee seemed to be in better spirits. He was much more upbeat and seemed more interested in Belle again. He seemed to have finally forgiven her for the miscarriage. In April 2013, Gee arranged to meet Belle for lunch but then phoned to say he couldn't make it. Could they meet for dinner instead? At dinner she waited for him but he didn't show up. She called and texted but got no reply. Days went by. Belle was frantically worried that he had been in an accident or become ill.

Belle had no number or address for Gee's father. She had never met any of his friends so had no one she could contact to ask where he was. She knew he worked at St Christopher's Children's Hospital but didn't know in which department or who she could ask about it. Finally Belle went to the apartment but the code for the main entrance didn't work. She wondered if he had left her and was just ghosting her. She hung around and waited for someone to come into the building, and seeing the key in her hand they let her through the main door. She went up to the apartment and found that the key didn't work. Belle decided that he must have moved back to England – something he had threatened to do when depressed – either that or he might have gone off and committed suicide.

That is how it was left for Belle. Two years went by and she had no word, no reassurance that he was even alive, and no closure, until one evening when she was offered an extra shift at work. Getting changed after her shower, she sat down on the bed, sitting on the remote control. The channel changed and there on TV was *NBC Dateline*. She let it run as she continued to get dressed. The interviewees were talking about a man called William Allen Jordan, a bigamist and con man as well as a convicted paedophile. 'That guy sounds like a jerk!' she said out loud.

Whilst she was looking in the mirror putting on her make-up she spotted a photograph on TV in the reflection. Stunned, she turned around and stared at the television. The man looked like Gee, but it couldn't be him as this man had a different name. Belle picked up her phone and took a snapshot of the screen and texted it to her friend, asking, 'Does he look familiar?'

Immediately she got a reply. 'Is he trying to contact you again?'

'Oh my God, that really is him!' Belle replied and told her friend about the *NBC Dateline* programme.

Belle watched the broadcast and then looked Mischele up on Facebook and sent her a message. She didn't expect to get a response at all. To her surprise, Mischele wrote back immediately and they started a conversation.

After talking to Mischele, Belle talked to me as well. Belle was shocked to hear everything that had happened to Will Jordan's previous victims as well as the women whose experience with Gee had overlapped hers, including Mischele who had started seeing him in January 2013. She now knows of at least two other women who were in a relationship with Gee at the same time as she was. Belle had once woken up hearing a woman screaming on the phone. Even though Gee was in the living room and Belle was in the bedroom, she could hear the woman screeching. When she came through and asked who was on the phone, the woman screamed some more and then Gee hung up. He explained that it was his sister and she was unhappy about something to do with their parents. Belle had not fully believed him at the time but didn't have enough evidence to disbelieve him either. There was also a woman she had seen at the house Gee was doing up. When she had arrived to check on progress, a woman and child were inside with Gee. Belle called him and Gee came out saying that because of the money issues he couldn't afford for them to live there until later and meantime was planning to rent it out. The woman was a potential tenant and he said, 'Please don't ruin the deal for me.' Looking back, Belle thinks that the woman was probably living at the house with him.

Hindsight offers clarity. It was only when Belle was relating the full story to me that she realised that Will Jordan had probably drugged her that first night and most likely raped her. He comes across as a gentle man with such good manners and a pleasant demeanour that you simply would not expect it of him. He even made her feel guilty for passing out and she apologised for causing him any inconvenience. You do not expect someone to drug and rape you, then continue to behave in such a gentle manner, even continuing with the relationship. He wasn't exhibiting behaviour that would be perceived as threatening. What is more, with the benefit of 20/20 hindsight, she realised it was possible that he had planned the whole thing. He probably knew his 'favourite restaurant' would be closed and might even have booked the hotel room in advance.

During the first part of their relationship, someone was giving him money – large sums of cash at a time. Belle also wonders how on earth he got the St Christopher's scrubs and the patient records. They looked very real and she wonders now if he stole them.

As for being stopped by the police, Will clearly knows exactly what to say and to whom – including how to deal with policemen so they don't notice his lack of a driving licence. It doesn't always work, I know, because he has numerous charges against him for driving without a licence and without insurance, but it is interesting to have a witness as to how he sometimes gets away with it. Even the police are fooled by this consummate con man.

The apartment Will Jordan was living in was just across the road from where he was arrested in April 2014, captured by the press photographer in the police sting set up by Mischele.

Belle rarely dates nowadays and is still single. She also feels bad for anyone she does date because she gets nervous and starts to fact-check them. No one wants a girlfriend who wants to take their fingerprints and starts investigating them, but how are we all supposed to do our 'due diligence' otherwise? When you meet someone for the first time, you simply have to go on trust – every relationship is based on that.

Belle said, 'He's the strongest *punk* I know.' She described him as pure charisma, talking himself out of any situation. If you asked questions, he always had a ready and convincing answer, and there seemed to be evidence just lying around to verify what he was saying – like the patient records and bills on his office desk. She added, 'I think I must have known somewhere deep down that he was no good, which is why I never introduced him to my children. Something, some kind of spider sense, was jangling in my subconscious.' Gee would always play on her nursing and mothering instincts by accusing her of not trusting him, and this made her feel guilty.

Belle has not told her children about him yet, even though they are well into their teenage years now. She has kept it from most of her friends and family as well because she is embarrassed and not sure how to broach the subject. She has said that she will tell them all one day, and then laughed saying she might suggest they read this book first!

Facebook

Our group of victims was growing, and the new Facebook group was very useful. It let us talk to each other from all over the world. We shared stories and experiences and talked about the ongoing issues of recovery, as well as sharing hopes and fears. It was hugely supportive for all of us to be able to talk without needing to explain ourselves – and specifically without any kind of judgement. We all knew exactly what we had been through.

From prison, Will Jordan applied for a special programme called the 'Intensive Supervision Program' or ISP. This was created to help those serving a minimum amount of jail time who could be released before being eligible for parole. It allows some offenders to serve the rest of their sentence outside the traditional prison setting but under strict supervision. The idea is that non-violent prisoners may be better served working as volunteers in churches or in schools rather than sitting in prison. It would mean that Will Jordan could carry out his sentence in the community instead of in jail.

Mischele told us that she had been informed of his application and was asked if she had anything she wanted the panel to know before they discussed the matter? We were all astonished that they were even considering his application, given his history and the paedophilia conviction in the UK.

We worried that if Mischele alone wrote about her objections to the judge in his case, it might be dismissed as being only one person's perspective. So instead, we *all* wrote to the judge, from Scotland, England,

Mexico and the USA. Eight of us wrote to the court – women standing together in unison to support Mischele's testimony.

It worked and his application was denied.

As a group, it was incredibly validating to work together to stop him in his tracks.

The membership of our Facebook group has ebbed and flowed over the years with some members moving on when they felt the time was right. Each time we check with the members before inviting a new victim to join – and talk to them on video chat beforehand to make sure they are not Will Jordan himself posing as a victim!

◆ ◆ ◆

All this time the other wife was still phoning me and we talked regularly. However, she was also keeping the lines of communication open with Will Jordan and his family. She could never seem to let go entirely. In 2014, her eldest son, who was now twenty-one, got in touch and asked if he could talk to me.

As an adult he had a right to the truth and I made a promise to my own children in 2006 that I would never lie to anyone. I told him that I was happy to speak to him and answer any questions he had, but that I would not lie to his mum if she asked me about it.

Enough damage had been done by lies and deceit and I wanted nothing further to do with Will Jordan's lies.

The son wanted to know my side of things, so I answered every one of his questions honestly and completely, exactly as I had done with my own children. He asked each of his questions politely and listened calmly to the answers, asking in detail what Will Jordan had done to us and to others.

Then he asked, 'Do you think he's a sociopath?'

'No, I think he's a psychopath,' I answered. 'When I first wrote my book, the definitions were slightly different and seem to have changed over the years. A psychopath is born and a sociopath is made by their experiences in childhood. I think he was born this way, though possibly not improved by his upbringing. Either way, I don't think he has any empathy or emotion for others. I don't think he is capable of love.'

He thanked me politely and said goodbye.

Shortly after my conversation with him, I had a furious call from his mother. She asked if he had called me and as promised I told her the truth. She was incensed.

'How would you feel if I told *your* children that their father was a sociopath?' she growled at me in fury.

'They'd probably tell you that he's actually a psychopath and then tell you what the difference is!' I replied.

She was not amused.

After eight years of talking several times a week on the phone, she cut ties with me altogether. She also fell out with Mischele because her son had spoken to Mischele as well. She said she wanted nothing to do with me or my children any more. After that she left our group and blocked us all on Facebook.

Every so often she unblocks me and sends a message demanding that I stop talking about Will Jordan, that I take any mention of her out of my book and let the subject drop. Sadly, she has also persuaded her children to cut ties with mine. I hope that one day they get in touch again as this is a source of sadness, particularly to Eilidh who had a good relationship with them all.

I still feel sorry for the other wife though. I don't think she has dealt with the situation and still feels embarrassed that anyone might find out she is connected to him in any way. I don't think her children have ever had a chance to deal with the situation at all, and they somehow feel that it is my fault that he had to leave their family. I also think she still feels he loved her and believes him when he tells her that she was special to him – something that would make her vulnerable to him again in the future.

CAN'T SAVE EVERYONE

After Mischele and my *NBC Dateline* episode in 2015, whilst Will Jordan was in jail, we were also contacted by a woman who was very worried about a relative. It was one of Will Jordan's younger girlfriends/victims. The woman was distraught because her relative, Rachel, had met Will Jordan on a website called PregnantDating.com before giving birth to a daughter (apparently not by Will Jordan) in 2012. The woman asked me and Mischele to talk to Rachel to help her understand who she was involved with.

We both spoke to Rachel and introduced her to the Facebook group. Rachel was hesitant and nervous and kept saying that she wanted to reserve judgement. For a while we thought we had got through to her. She never seemed to be fully on board though and was clearly torn.

Because Will was in jail, we kept in touch with Rachel. Somehow he managed to send her flowers from prison – possibly through his parents. He would write to her and send her love letters, telling her how she was his 'one'. Even when she moved out of New Jersey to Vermont, his letters followed.

◆ ◆ ◆

In 2015, Mischele and I tried to get Will Jordan back on the Megan's Law register, this time with Mischele talking directly to the New Jersey State Police while I was once more talking to authorities in the UK.

I made an appointment with my Member of Parliament, Ian Murray, and took all the newspaper articles as well as my book to the meeting. Ian sat and listened attentively to my story and at the end said with some astonishment, 'Well, that is the first time I have had anyone use the words "CIA", "psychopath" and "paedophile" all in one session!'

Ian was marvellous. He helped by writing to the Secretary of State, asking him to send Will Jordan's criminal conviction record to the New Jersey State Police in order for them to put him on the Megan's Law register as a sex offender.

Weeks later he got a reply that essentially said 'No'. They said that under the data protection laws they could not give *me* his details. We replied, reiterating that we wanted the records sent to the New Jersey State Police and *not* to me, but got no further response.

Meanwhile Mischele got a similar runaround. No one seemed interested. The New Jersey State Police had a convicted paedophile in their area and did not bother requesting the information so he could be put on the register. It still astounds me that something so simple is not done out of sheer lack of effort. And considering that the man targets single mothers, it is very worrying.

Mischele had better luck with changing the law though. A US Senator became interested in her fight to make sexual assault by deception easier and clearer to prosecute. I have not covered much of Mischele's story and won't go into detail about her legal fight because Mischele is writing her own book about the experience, not just her relationship with Will Jordan but spying on him, her interaction with his parents whom she knew well, and setting up the police sting. Once Will Jordan was in jail, Mischele started a blog charting her ongoing battle to change the law whilst also being a working single mother. It is inspiring, and I'm looking forward to reading the whole story from her perspective.

Psychopath Nights

Jon Ronson and I kept in touch over the years and in January 2016 he invited me to do a live show with him as the finale of *Five Nights with Jon Ronson* in London's Leicester Square Theatre. The show was called *The Psychopath Night* and it was not only sold out but had a waiting list of 144 people, so Jon decided to take the show on tour. In November 2016 we did a two-week tour of the UK and Ireland. Every event was sold out.

The show had a simple format. Jon would talk about researching his book *The Psychopath Test* and then ask me on stage, where he would interview me about my story. We had a rough routine and various places where we would both inject humour into the conversation, but the interview was not scripted at all. On hearing my story, the audience usually gasped and laughed on cue. One reviewer for the *York Press* wrote, 'suffice to say the collective thud of jaws dropping as one to the floor was a sound to behold.'

The show continued with Jon talking about his book and his experience with researching psychopaths, as well as talking about the madness industry. He then brought on his second guest Dr Eleanor Longden, an eminent psychologist who also happens to hear voices and had her own story to tell about her experiences in psychiatric care. The second half of the show was just the three of us onstage taking questions from the audience.

The first show was on the evening of Tuesday 8 November 2016, and it went amazingly well. It was the same day as the US presidential election and we were asked questions about Donald Trump as people laughed at the possibility of his being elected to the office of the President of the United States of America. Clearly that couldn't happen. It was unimaginable. But after the show I was asked if I thought Trump was a psychopath.

'No, there's a big issue with trying to diagnose people from afar but from what I know of him I would be more likely to say he's a malignant narcissist,' I answered.

'What's the difference?' I was asked.

The difference between psychopaths and sociopaths is nature and nurture. Psychopaths are born with no empathic responses, and sociopaths are made by society but the results are the same as both are lacking in any chemical empathic response for anyone, *including* themselves. As already mentioned, empathic people care about their future selves rather like they do other people, as was demonstrated by the electric shock test. So psychopaths and sociopaths can live moment to moment without caring about what their future self might have to endure (pain, prison, homelessness, etc.).

Narcissists, on the other hand, lack any chemical empathic response for anyone *except* themselves. So their whole world revolves around them and anyone they consider part of themselves (such as an obedient child or spouse – who generally realise that if they don't toe the line they will be cut off with the speed and efficiency of a guillotine). A *malignant* narcissist takes it one step further in that the narcissist will actively go out of their way to destroy someone they believe has slighted them or not given them the godlike status they feel they deserve. A component of malignant narcissism is sadism – and that is not limited to causing others pain but also taking glee in the suffering of their perceived 'enemies' (in other words, those who don't worship them or people who have stood up against them in the past).

Apaths are another category, and are also interesting in that they are people with a conscience and with empathy, but who dull their own emotional responses around a psychopath or narcissist so as to be able to work for them. They are sometimes called 'flying monkeys' because (whether out of fear or greed) they do their master's or mistress's bidding without feeling for their victims.

To me Donald Trump shows every sign of a malignant narcissist – someone who clearly demonstrates a lack of empathy, pathological lying, a grandiose sense of self-worth and the like, but also paranoia (all those conspiracy theories), aggression, boastfulness, belief in his own fantasies (his claim that the crowd at his inauguration was the largest 'of all time' is a good example), and exaggeration of his own abilities and status ('stable genius'!). What's more, if you listen to Trump speak, he uses exaggeration, reframing, projection and has actually made the term 'word salad' commonplace!

As a Scot I had been exposed to Donald Trump's treatment of the people around his Scottish golf courses and how he had tried to bulldoze over the locals to get what he seemed to feel entitled to. I could think of no one *less* suited to becoming the President of the United States and feared what he might do (particularly with access to a nuclear arsenal) if elected. Especially if he did not get everything his own way!

That evening, after the first *Psychopath Night* with Jon Ronson, I watched from my hotel room with increasing horror as the election results rolled in. Like millions of others around the world I was aghast to find that Donald Trump had actually won the 2016 presidential election.

The second *Psychopath Night* show was a different beast altogether. The audience were in shock – as were we all. The mood in the theatre seemed to be one of total disbelief as people tried to absorb the second extraordinary result of the year (the first being the Brexit vote in the UK). It seemed that the world was going mad – quite an appropriate setting for a sell-out show about the madness industry and psychopathy!

There was a lot of talk about what had happened as well as discussing the 'Goldwater Rule' (the informal name of the medical ethics rule which states it is unethical for psychiatrists to give a professional opinion about public figures whom they have not examined in person, nor received consent to discuss!) We did point out that as non-professionals in the field we are not bound by the Goldwater Rule. I strongly feel there is a more urgent requirement which is the duty to warn others about people who are genuinely unstable, putting the safety of society first. Interestingly, a group of psychiatrists and clinical psychologists came out in 2017 stating that the 'Duty to Warn' in the case of Donald Trump overcame all restraints of the Goldwater Rule.

John Gartner, a practising psychologist, went public with his statements. As founder of 'Duty to Warn PAC' (a political action committee working to raise awareness about the danger to the USA and the world posed by Donald Trump), his statements in *Forbes Magazine* in February 2017 were damning. Gartner said that America had had lots of presidents with mental health issues that 'wouldn't disqualify and might even enhance' their ability to perform their duties. But, he said, the Trump situation is 'from a psychiatric point of view the absolute worst-case scenario . . . if I were to take the DSM (Diagnostic and Statistical Manual of Mental Disorders) and try to create a Frankenstein's monster of the most dangerous and destructive leader and had freedom to create any combination of diagnosis and symptoms', Trump would be the result.

He went on to say that in Trump's case it is not a single condition at work but rather that Trump shows a quartet of conditions that add up to malignant narcissism, a term that was originally devised to characterise Hitler. Garner stated the four conditions as 'narcissism, paranoia and antisocial personality disorder, with a dash of sadism thrown in'.

I loved doing the show with Jon Ronson. The stories he tells are funny because they recognise the vulnerability in the human condition whilst also being shockingly recognisable. I sat backstage each night and laughed at each story he related even though I had heard it over and over again. We did the tour again in 2017 in different cities, and bigger venues (up to 2,000 people in the audience) which was again sold out everywhere we went. It was phenomenal being able to sit onstage and make people laugh about such a serious subject. It was amazing as well to hear 2,000 people gasp – interestingly enough there were certain points in the show at which the women gasped in unison and other points where the men did, clearly showing what different aspects they each found shocking. I felt completely comfortable talking about the issues, something that often surprises people, but the more I did it, the more comfortable I felt. I also found the show quite cathartic; talking about my story over and over again each night helped me to see it for what it was, something that happened in the past.

My fascination with psychopaths and narcissists grew as I wanted to understand more and more about the subject, and the questions that the audience asked in the second part of the show helped me to expand on that curiosity, especially when they asked questions I had not heard or thought about before.

People asked me about the other victims and if we kept in touch and were surprised to find out about the private Facebook group where we can all chat and keep tabs on what Will Jordan is doing. They asked about the children and whether they talk to each other, about Will Jordan's parents and if I thought they were psychopaths too. (I suspect that his father might be, or at the very least an apath.)

I remember one chap on the last night asking if I would consider marrying again and I replied that we had only just met but if he was interested he should keep in touch. The audience roared with laughter.

Opposites Attract

I had spent six years with a man who was severely psychopathic and the question 'Why me?' reverberated around my mind. How had this all happened? What was it about *me* that made me an attractive target? There had to be some reason, something about my past that made me the perfect mark. Will Jordan had crawled under my defences and into my life and pushed his way under my skin like a poisonous splinter. Day by day, pushing further in, bonding me to him through love-bombing, gaslighting me into distrusting myself, and using reframing, projection and word salad to keep me hooked – every manipulation technique available to brainwash me into compliance. Looking back, it was still hard to comprehend how I was so totally taken in. I needed to understand my own role in all of this. I needed to know what made me accept his behaviour when others wouldn't have done so.

It's disturbing how many of the victims of psychopaths I have talked to were also previously abused in early life or young adulthood, and I wondered whether there was a correlation. I was abused as a child by a family 'friend' called Jimmy, who used to come over and play hide-and-seek with my three older siblings and me. He always used to find me first. I participated in his 'game' and enjoyed the adult attention. Being the youngest of four children, it was nice to have an adult solely focused on me. I was four years old.

I can now see how Jimmy groomed me, see how he tested the waters by exposing himself. He stood in the hallway with his penis hanging out of his trousers and his hands on his hips. I giggled as I asked what 'that' was. As a result, I became a target.

If I had pointed and said I could see his 'penis', he would have zipped up and put it away. Then he would have mentioned to my parents that I had walked into the bathroom on him and he was worried I might have seen something whilst he was taking a pee, thereby neutralising anything I might have reported back to them. Paedophiles don't target children who have the language to describe what has happened to them.

Once targeted, it became his regular game. I would hide and Jimmy would come in and shut the door. It became a secret, a game between us that was not to be talked about – because I would be in trouble if I did. It only ended when I was about six years old when my twelve-year-old brother stopped him at the door. The man had been coming around too often when my parents were out. I think he was caught abusing another child and he never came back again. What happened to me stopped when I was about six but it didn't start to trouble me until I was a teenager. I understood the rude jokes too easily, people started to talk about sex and I remembered things I shouldn't have. I started to realise that what had happened to me wasn't normal. Far worse was that I remembered enjoying the 'game', and that gave me a deep sense of shame and self-loathing.

I was diagnosed with dyslexia when I was thirteen, something that was quite newly being recognised in schools at the time. It helped to explain why I struggled in class but it didn't stop my classmates from moaning if I had to get up and read. I felt like I was less 'able' than the other students and when I did well, I assumed it was a fluke rather than through my skill. My feeling of being mentally subnormal combined with the self-loathing.

I used to cut myself or bite myself or burn myself when it got too bad. I used physical pain to blot out any emotions that rose to the surface. I also became very good at hiding what I'd done as well. I shrugged the injuries off as accidents and smiled sweetly at people as I related some story of how it had happened. I remember taking a piece of broken glass and scoring two crossed lines across the back of my left hand. When my sister Isobel saw it I told her I had fallen over on glass – she believed me even though it was an odd injury to have sustained from a fall.

I never attempted suicide. Although I didn't really care if I lived or died, I would never have done that to my family. I might not have cared about myself but I did care very deeply about them.

I don't really remember much about my childhood or my teenage years because I spent so much time acting a part and pretending that everything was OK. It worked sometimes. I was a good gymnast and a great musician. There are snapshots and pieces of memory, peaks appearing above the fog.

When I finally told someone and said the words out loud, I was seventeen years old.

I said simply, 'I was molested as a child.'

The friend I was with looked horrified and said, 'That must have been awful; you must have been terrified!'

There it was, the attitude I was to hear over and over again and the comment that made me believe I was an even more unworthy and unlovable person because I hadn't been terrified. Childline, the telephone line support organisation, had started as well as new national campaigns to save abused children, each campaign talking publicly about the abuse and horrors that happened to molested children. They all reinforced the fact that child abuse was a horrible thing and that I should have been petrified at the time. I should have found it awful and disgusting; I should have fought my abuser off and told my parents. But I hadn't. I had participated and joined in his game. Therefore, in my mind, I must have been as bad as him. I was as bad or worse than a paedophile. It was a horrible time. Saying the words out loud was like turning a key to a locked door inside my head. I recognised that behind that door was the monster part of me that I had shut away, and now it was clamouring to come out. It terrified me. I had to do everything I could to keep that door shut.

I had my first lover when I was eighteen and it felt like I was taking control back. I could use sex rather than letting sex use me. I could use sex instead of cutting myself. From then on, I was almost constantly in a couple and they were always quite highly sexual relationships. I rarely lost control though and although very good at sex I was not very good at relationships. When I started to open up and trust the man I was with, I would also start to push them away because quite simply I felt I was not worthy of love and therefore they were wrong to love me at all. I could only respect the men who disrespected me, because at least they knew who I really was and what I deserved.

I started a degree course in Creative and Performing Arts in 1983, and one day I met someone whose body language seemed familiar. I knew without her saying that she had been molested too but had never talked about it. So I told her my story instead, that I had been abused, and a bit about what had happened. She opened up to me and told me her story in return. It helped me so much just to know I had not been alone. After that I would recognise more and more people, and started to talk to those I knew who had also experienced childhood sexual abuse. Finally I instinctively knew the time was right and admitted to someone that the hardest thing to overcome was the fact that I had enjoyed it. Her eyes opened wide and she lit up like a light bulb. She felt the same way. It was not just me. Over the years I heard more and more people say the same thing and each one had felt unlovable and dirty because of it.

I graduated from college in 1987 and got a 2:1 in my BA Hons Creative and Performing Arts degree. I had expected to fail and as a result had not really worked as hard as I should have, so the result came as rather a surprise.

As I got older, I came to understand and to forgive myself for having participated in the paedophile's game. It took a few more years of talking to people and writing about it, but gradually a door opened up inside me and I could see there wasn't a monster inside the room at all. It was a little four-year-old girl sitting on the floor against the back wall. Her legs bent and her head hidden in the folded arms resting on her knees. All around her was dust and cobwebs and she didn't move or talk but just sat there muffling her tears. I was no longer frightened of her; I just felt an overwhelming sorrow for having trapped her there for so long and wanted to set her free.

Then one day when I was in my mid-twenties, I woke up and sat bolt upright in bed. I don't know what had happened or if I had had a dream or something, but I felt a huge change. Almost like a hallucination, I witnessed the door of the room in my head swing open and hit the wall behind it. The room crumbled to dust and the wind blew through it in a gust. The girl was gone.

I finally realised on an instinctive level that I was not to blame. That I was an innocent child who didn't have the knowledge or understanding to stand up to an adult who was abusing me. I also realised that what he had done to me ended when I was six years old, and everything that had happened since I had done to myself. I had been a victim but I wasn't going to be any more. I chose to love that little girl inside me, to nurture her and accept her, for every wonderful thing that she was and not to punish her for the crimes against her.

Having accepted and forgiven myself for being caught by a paedophile, the next step was to forgive him. That took a while, but I knew that hating Jimmy or being angry would just hurt me more and I decided that I wanted to be happy. As someone said to me, hating someone else is like taking poison and expecting them to die. So I talked to a lot of people and I read a lot of books – I became fascinated by psychology and interested in why people like Jimmy abuse others.

I found out that people are not born paedophiles and usually become that way because they were abused as children themselves. Rather than come to terms with it, they take on the role of abuser instead. I decided that my abuser was not evil, but just damaged. I figured that most people who hurt others were probably victims themselves at one point or another. Nowhere, in all my reading, was there ever a mention of a paedophile being a psychopath or sociopath.

To forgive my abuser I had to have empathy for him as an abuse victim himself. I had to have the ability to feel and imagine that he had emotion. I could cognitively and emotionally empathise with him because I had been an abuse victim myself. I had struggled and fought against my own abuse by hurting myself, he had gone another way and hurt others instead.

I had initially met Ross (Robyn's biological father) in my early twenties when I played bodhran (a traditional Celtic drum) for fun on the live music scene in Edinburgh. I was predominantly a pianist but it was rather difficult to carry a piano around the different pubs we played in socially so I learnt to play the bodhran instead.

Ross was a professional singer and guitarist with the most amazing voice – a talent that captivated audiences wherever he went. He was a damaged soul and a real man's man, and that all came out in his singing. I think I fell in love with his voice more than anything. We dated for a while and then I found out one day that he was two-timing me with another girl. I dumped him immediately. He tried numerous times to get me back and I just brushed him off. I had to stop seeing my friends and leave the social scene that we shared because it became too difficult and uncomfortable to be near him. Eventually I heard he moved away.

Then in 1997 he returned, a new man. He had cleaned up his act, stopped drinking so much and told me he had stopped taking drugs. (I had known that he smoked weed but hadn't been aware that he'd been taking a lot of speed and cocaine before he left Edinburgh.)

Gradually, we became friends again and saw a bit of each other.

I'd been dating a ranger with whom I was very much in love, but it just couldn't work, and when it broke up Ross was there for me. He held me and told me everything would be OK. He never made a pass at me or tried to seduce me. He just behaved like a great friend for over a year. However, he would tell me over and over again that he had cleaned up his act to win me back, that he was in love with me and wanted to spend the rest of his life with me. His actions that year left me in no doubt that he was genuine and finally I decided tentatively to trust him. Initially I just wanted to take it slow but as soon as we started getting close he started to talk about having a baby. He worked nights as a live musician and I worked days as a business adviser, so we would each have time to look after the baby, he would say.

I said no, but maybe sometime. I was not particularly the motherly type and wasn't sure if I ever wanted to have kids – certainly not yet. But I was getting on and at thirty-three, I felt I would soon have to make a decision one way or the other.

By this time I was working as a business development adviser for the Scottish Enterprise Network, providing business development advice to help local small companies expand and grow. One of my clients was a fertility expert and I broached the subject with her.

'Oh, don't worry about it too much,' she said. 'At your age it's likely to take at least a year to get pregnant anyway.'

So I relaxed a little and when Ross next brought it up I had a moment of weakness. I flippantly said we could let fate decide. It only took that one shot!

So I was pregnant. Almost immediately, Ross seemed to go off me although he was over the moon about the idea of becoming a dad. And he didn't want to have sex any more, almost like his goal had already been achieved. I seem to remember reading an article about Elvis not wanting to touch his wife when she was pregnant and thought it possible that Ross felt the same way. It was a strange time. Ross was there and still very loving but he was also quite removed. He didn't want to talk about the future at all.

I knew Ross had had a rough time with his own father and subsequent stepfathers – but that is not my story to tell.

So Ross was damaged, and I understood his conflicting emotions. I had a lot of empathy for him, but it was hard.

I went into labour at 7 a.m. on 14 February 1999. Ross had come home at 3 a.m. and brought me flowers for Valentine's Day. The joke was that my contractions had started because I had gone into shock at the romantic gesture.

When I felt the contractions start I let Ross sleep a bit. By 8 a.m. they were stronger and only a few minutes apart. I called my lovely mother, who was coming over to take us to the maternity hospital, then I woke Ross who was bemused and a bit annoyed at my choice of timing. He groggily got out of bed and tagged along.

In the words of the midwife, the birth was 'absolutely textbook'.

As Robyn was placed beside me, still attached, I looked into her dark eyes with total wonder and in that moment understood what real true love was. Here was this tiny creature, confused and fragile, totally dependent on me. The bond was instant.

Ross liked being a dad but he was not prepared for it emotionally at all. He thought life could continue as it had before, just with a new addition. For three months I nursed Robyn and when my maternity leave was up, I went back to work. Initially Ross looked after Robyn during the day but he found it very difficult. He worked playing music in pubs most evenings until midnight but then would hang around having a couple of pints with his mates until three or four in the morning.

He would then come home and watch TV for an hour or so. I left for work at 8 a.m. and occasionally found him still up.

I would come home at lunchtime to feed Robyn and a couple of times found Ross asleep on the couch with Robyn bawling in her cot. It became clear that he couldn't manage and he refused to change his lifestyle.

I tried reasoning with Ross but he was far better at arguments than me. He didn't care what he said and would be as hurtful as possible – calling me all the names under the sun – because if I was upset then I couldn't argue the point. I never felt physically threatened by him but he could verbally dominate me easily, screaming abuse for the smallest of things. I was totally convinced that I had to hold my family together and that Robyn needed her father around as much as she needed me.

I signed Robyn up to a nursery three days a week, meaning he only had to look after her two days a week (as I was home at the weekends). But things just got worse from then on. Ross became less and less engaged and more aggressive as time went on.

I would still have to get up at night when Robyn woke up and cried, even if Ross was awake and watching TV. He insisted that I had the night shift and he had the day shift even though I was working all day and now doing overtime at the weekend to pay for the nursery hours.

Ross became more and more nasty and unpleasant until one day I was so incensed at his insults that I hit him over and over again. He just laughed at me and didn't even hold his hands up to defend himself. When I stopped he said, 'Don't you realise, Mary, that I am *never* going to leave you. I will never let you tell our daughter that I walked out. When will you realise that things are just going to continue getting worse until you *throw* me out!'

It snapped me awake. I had believed so strongly that I had to keep my little family together, that I hadn't seen he was deliberately trying to make things difficult. I realised I was wrong, that I had been teaching my daughter the kind of relationship she should look for, just like Ross had been taught.

Robyn was only just nine months old and I wanted to give her a better life than that, so I told Ross to leave.

He went willingly.

Ross was a sporadic father at best after he left, but I found life a lot easier without him. Although I had to do everything myself, at least I didn't feel angry at having to do so. I just got on with it and found being in control was better. Robyn was a delight and I very quickly got used to it being just the two of us.

I vowed that I would never let a man be aggressive towards me again, nor would I allow anyone to raise their voice to me like Ross had. I was happy. I had a good job, my own home, money in the bank and a loving family. I didn't mind being single – once I got past my own old-fashioned prejudice against single parents.

Having a daughter had taught me what real love was and from now on I was going be the good example for her to follow. If I wanted her to be happy I had to show her the way. I stayed single and happy for a year, then a friend suggested I try Internet dating – a very new innovation at the time. I was intrigued and prepared to dip a toe in the water, but was not desperately craving a new relationship. Unlike before, I didn't feel the need to have a man around. I felt whole for the first time in my life. It would, however, be nice for Robyn to have a good, kind, loving and attentive stepdad, if one could be found.

That is when I met Will Jordan.

◆ ◆ ◆

I told Will Jordan about my abuse as a child, about my journey of discovery and about my forgiveness of my abuser. I told him all about my relationship with Ross, how I had found his aggression intolerable and would never stand for anyone raising their voice to me like that again. As a result Will Jordan became the epitome of calm around me. He became everything that Ross was not: calm, gentle, loving, attentive, seemingly selfless and kind, self-assured and emotionally intelligent.

He used every detail about my past to manipulate me, including telling me that as part of an intelligence operation, he had gone under-cover to infiltrate a sex offender prison and catch a particular paedophile ring that was operating in the UK.

I had given it all to him on a platter by telling him so much about me early on.

I'm an empathic person. I can tell when others are in pain; I notice body language and speech patterns which tell me if someone is hurting or damaged. I not only understand other people's pain but can actually feel it in my body. It was that empathy that made me open up and talk to other victims about my abuse. I had empathised with and forgiven my childhood sexual abuser, and I empathised with Ross, even when he was actively trying to make things bad for me. And it was my empa-thy that made it so hard for me to comprehend that a person like Will Jordan could be so wholly without conscience, remorse or emotional response to others.

That word kept coming back and back into my head. Empathy.

I had thought I knew what it meant – the ability to understand and share the feelings of another – and more importantly I thought that everyone but psychopaths had it! But then I started to look a little deeper. There is research done on empathy but not as much as done on psychopathy, I suppose because empaths are not dangerous to society per se. However, there are tests you can do to measure your empathy level and each one I did came out showing I was 'highly empathic'.

I started to think about the other victims and suddenly realised that something we all had in common was that we are all empaths. A lot of the victims are in caring or nurturing jobs – nurses, social work-ers, teachers – and a lot of them had come through previous abusive relationships, childhood abuse or emotional trauma. But they had come through it and risen from the ashes – just like I had done.

Empathy explains why the victims fell for Will Jordan's stories about being infertile, or his lies about having been abused as a child himself. It explains how he can rationalise away some of the things he does by making it sound like he is in distress, or even inflicting pain and damage on himself.

I had spent so long researching psychopaths that I had missed something vital; I had assumed everyone who was not on the scale of psychopathy was empathic. But that's not the case. There's a scale of empathy just like there's a scale of psychopathy. And I suspect that the more of an empath you are, the more of a psychopath you might be targeted by – as they say, 'opposites attract'.

People with antisocial disorders are low empaths; in other words, they don't care about anyone except themselves. Put simply, 'using and abusing' leaves no imprint on their conscience. Conversely, their victims are often high empaths or emotionally sensitive: people who feel genuine pain when others are hurt or in trouble. Psychopaths love these empathic types because their inherent caring makes them not give up easily – even when the psychopath begins exhibiting disturbing behaviour. Someone who is not so empathic is more likely to leave a man who starts to show signs of aggression, addiction or lying, whilst a highly empathic woman will instead think that she can help or even save the psychopath. As a result she stays and becomes even more bonded and involved with her abuser, becoming even more convinced that her help is needed, despite troubling or escalating behaviour on his part.

Sandra L. Brown, who wrote *Women Who Love Psychopaths*, was asked how psychopaths choose their targets and she said:

> 'I've asked men like this how they pick their targets and they say they'll tell a sad story about early childhood abuse to see someone's reaction. They're looking for someone

very compassionate who is willing to problem solve, who will be all "oh, that's terrible, oh my god, you should get some help", because that woman has to get hooked into their storyline and be willing to rescue their ass over and over again. The woman who says, "good luck with that" – he's not going to be chasing her into a corner.'

Women who have high levels of empathy as well as compassion, trust, tolerance and attachment, simply do not see the red flags that others might until it is too late. Once a woman like this gets involved with someone, no matter how toxic the person turns out to be, it's very difficult for her to disengage.

It isn't possible to stop being an empath, and I would never want to, but I can work on emotional control and choose who I share my empathy with. I have accepted who I am and have learnt how to say 'no' to people who are psychological and emotional vampires. As someone once told me, 'Remember that "No" is a complete sentence and doesn't need any clarification.' Although life is not always easy, I am proud of who I am. Will Jordan may have used my empathy against me, but I still see it as a superpower. I just need to learn to control it better.

Imposters

Whenever I had passed an exam or had done well at something I always felt it must be a fluke or a mistake. It took a long time for me to realise that I wasn't stupid and when I finally did, I wanted to know why I had felt like that before. I found out that it's something ironically called 'impostor syndrome' and it is defined as a feeling that you don't deserve your accomplishments, have doubts about inadequacy, and fear being found out as a fraud (even though you know you have done everything right).

I read that 70% of people suffer the syndrome at some point in their lives and I made a conscious decision to reject impostor syndrome altogether after that. However, it does still raise its head occasionally, particularly when I'm at book industry events amongst traditionally published authors, all of whom I perceive as being more valid and successful than me, although now I also realise most of them are thinking the same as me! Once I started talking openly about impostor syndrome I could see how common it is. It's also something that a manipulative person will use against their victim. If a toxic person can tap into their target's impostor syndrome, they can more easily control them.

I can imagine that it must be so easy – and probably really clear to these kinds of people – to use that insecurity. A small comment or perceived criticism of something the victim was starting to feel confidence about. A question of 'Did you do that all yourself?', which might from the outside seem an innocent statement (and in some cases look to be phrased as a compliment) but in fact is designed to play on a person's insecurity and put the victim down.

I remembered how Will Jordan made me feel – that I could only really succeed with him beside me, that without him I would be nothing. I don't remember the actual words he used but do remember that I constantly felt I had to live up to his expectations of me, which in itself meant I had low expectations of myself. I do remember him saying things like 'I only ever wanted to be the wind beneath your wings', which seems on the surface to be a nice thing to say but in fact implies a lack of ability to fly on your own.

Then I was reminded about the four 'control dramas' I was taught about during a work team-training day many years ago. These are four roles that people (not necessarily just psychopaths and narcissists) use to control other people's emotions in a subconscious way. They are the 'Interrogator', the 'Intimidator', the 'Aloof' and the 'Poor Me'.

Most normal young people use a control drama to get attention until they become more self-aware. Teenagers can often be 'Aloof' or 'Poor Me' and can move into 'Interrogator' and 'Intimidator' when they don't get what they want. Gradually though, they learn that they don't need to control other people but only themselves. Toxic people, however, just carry on learning how to perfect the techniques.

Will Jordan was expert in using all four dramas on me. He was subtle about it though – as most toxic people are.

The 'Interrogator' asks a question and then criticises the answer so that you become careful about what you say around them. For instance they might ask:

'How was work?'

'OK, but my boss was in a bad mood.'

'Oh, did you do something to annoy them?'

This makes the respondent question themselves. The easiest and possibly most subtle way I remember Will Jordan doing this was just to say 'Really?' after I had answered a personal question. For example:

'What's your favourite movie?'

'*The Shawshank Redemption.*'

'Really?' He would then pause (to make me feel uncomfortable and judged), followed a few seconds later with a casual warm smile, saying, 'Well, it is a very popular choice!'

The victim is left feeling like they have somehow made a fool of themselves, yet still feeling that the toxic perpetrator has been kind to them and let them off the hook. It plays heavily on a person's impostor syndrome and their fear of looking foolish for having poor judgement.

The 'Intimidator' usually controls the drama by being aggressive, creating fear directly or indirectly. Will Jordan was never aggressive towards me directly – to be honest, he knew that if he even raised his voice to me in anger I would leave immediately because of my bad experiences with Ross. That's a 'deal-breaker' for me. So he was always calm and never angry around me, but instead created intimidation through external forces. He persuaded me I was in real danger from 'unsavouries', people who had discovered his true identity and were threatening me and the children. He covertly controlled the drama through intimidation.

The 'Aloof' controls the energy around them by retreating into themselves and shutting down so that people will ask what is wrong and pay attention to them because they seem worried and confused.

Again, Will Jordan did this from the start of our relationship, not only retreating but entirely disappearing. He left me worried as to whether he was alive or not almost daily.

The 'Poor Me' tells a sob story of woe that may or may not be true. It grabs the attention by getting people to focus on what is upsetting the controller. Will Jordan did this when I was giving birth to our first child. He told me he was trapped in a war-torn country and damaged his feet intentionally to prove it so that I would focus on his supposed emotional and physical trauma rather than his being absent for the birth of his child.

It is difficult to deal with anyone who is using control dramas. There is no positive way to control other people because we are meant to focus on controlling ourselves rather than manipulating others. Good people do not have to control other people's emotions.

◆ ◆ ◆

Psychopaths groom their victims in a very similar way to paedophiles. They slowly hook you in, play on your empathy, manipulate your emotions and then undermine the foundations of your self-belief, self-esteem and self-confidence.

I understand that Will Jordan was clever but I am too. I understand that he was manipulative and callous but it is his total lack of empathy for another person that is so alien and difficult for an empath like me to comprehend.

In 2010, I read a research report called *Psychopathic Traits and Perceptions of Victim Vulnerability* by Sarah Wheeler which showed that the more psychopathic a person is, the better they are at spotting a potential victim, even just by their body language. This body language is incredibly subtle though; the study showed that psychopathic muggers can look at the way you walk and instinctively pick up on the length of a stride, how high you lift your feet and even how you shift your weight to identify how confident you are, and therefore whether to mug you or not. Psychopaths don't even have to think about it. They just target vulnerable people who are empathic – kind, understanding, accepting – and use those traits against them. I had thought I was keeping myself safe online by spending time getting to know Will Jordan through our long and intimate emails. The truth was that he was using that time to learn all about me, what motivated me, how accepting I was, and how empathic I was. Then, when he finally met me, he took that a step further by analysing my body language. And being unaware, I walked straight into his trap.

I suspect that younger, more inexperienced psychopaths target socially submissive, not particularly outgoing or worldly victims through body language such as lack of eye contact, fidgeting and avoidance of large gestures when shifting position. This serves a double purpose because the victims themselves are ill-equipped to resist the predator, and are so traumatised afterwards that they won't even speak out about their experiences. It leaves the predator free to move on to the next victim. More experienced psychopaths would get bored of this pretty quickly though, and target more challenging victims – stronger, more worldly and more confident, people who will push them to their limits and hone their skills even more.

Suddenly I realised that there is a reason that psychopaths seem to be the most charming people, certainly at the beginning of a relationship. They are the ones who sweep us off our feet and seem to know exactly what to say and when to say it. They appear magically and instinctively to know how to get under our skin and make us comfortable, so we relax, let our guards down and let them into our lives.

It is not magic though, nor is it purely instinctive. It's far simpler than that.

As teenagers and in our early twenties, most of us experiment with flirting and dating. You see a guy or a girl that you like and build up the courage to talk to them. It is nerve-wracking because of the potential humiliation and embarrassment of rejection. Rejection takes its toll on us emotionally, making us wary of approaching others. It may take a few days, weeks, months or even years before we build up the courage to risk putting ourselves 'out there' again. As a result, we select those we are attracted to very carefully and guard ourselves against the emotional pain of further rejection.

Psychopaths, sociopaths and narcissists are not encumbered by hurt feelings or embarrassment. If rejected, they simply shrug it off and move immediately onto the next person they are attracted to, each time learning from the rejection like a computer program. They can target dozens in one night until a strategy works. Over the course of just a couple of years they can target thousands of people in this way, never feeling upset or embarrassed about a rejection. Eventually they acquire a full database of how to approach shy people, how to approach the life-and-soul-of-the-party, how to approach the single parents, the divorcee, the injured and the kind-hearted. They know exactly how to react in each given situation simply because they have experienced it many times before.

The psychopath's 'charm' is simply learnt behaviour from the sheer volume of encounters they have had. They know what works with each person and can adapt quickly to accommodate what it is that *we* want. They reflect our desires and provide us with tried and tested techniques to win us over. They look like they are handing us their hearts but in reality it's an act which has been polished over time, indistinguishable from the real thing and impossible for any normal empathic person to know the difference. They appear to be more normal than normal people are, rather like a wax apple emulating the more imperfect real fruit.

We have to live on trust and be open to falling in love. Ultimately, it is only time that shows us the truth of someone's feelings. I wasn't wrong to fall in love with the person Will Jordan pretended to be. My feelings were genuine. It wasn't my fault that his were not, nor was I wrong to believe that someone loved me.

More and More Victims . . .

Will Jordan remained in jail until November 2017 when he was released early on 'good behaviour'. Shortly afterwards, Rachel disappeared and didn't reply to any messages. Interestingly, her relative, who had been so grateful for the support, also stopped replying to messages too.

Both Mischele and I assumed that Will Jordan had somehow persuaded them we were enemy agents and not to be trusted. Having seen him try to persuade Mischele on the video, I can just imagine how she was sucked in again.

It is sad but we can't save everyone. Both Mischele and I know how strong a pull he has and how convincing he can be. I know he will go to any lengths – even mutilating his own body – to provide evidence that what he says is true, so I can't blame the women who go back to him. However, I also know I have done everything I can to help.

The most recent victim to be in contact was a nineteen-year-old girl who was eight months pregnant by Will Jordan when she got in touch in July 2019. I will call her Jewel.

By 2018 Jewel had already had a hard life and suffered with anxiety disorders, self-harming and PTSD. She had pulled herself out of a horrible situation and decided to face the world again.

Jewel met Will Jordan in June 2018 on a dating website specifically for interracial couples and met in person for the first time on a beach in July 2018. He told her he was in his thirties even though he was actually fifty-four by then. He promised her the world, told her that she was his soulmate and asked her to move in to his apartment with him and his dad, all within only a few weeks of meeting. (It appears by that time that Will Jordan's mother was in a care home.) Jewel moved in with him within a couple of months. Will Jordan admitted to her that he had once been married to two women at the same time and implied that the women had taken their revenge by posting horrible stuff about him on the Internet. Jewel felt that he was being honest and up front, and therefore didn't feel the need to look him up online. As usual, he told her that he didn't have any children of his own with a hint that he had emotional baggage from that, and then he asked her to have a baby with him. Jewel didn't make a conscious decision to get pregnant but agreed that they would let nature take its course. Not surprisingly, given his clear fertility, she got pregnant very quickly and he almost immediately went cold and emotionless on her. It was mental and emotional torture for her and something I am sure he did deliberately.

As someone who suffered from PTSD and anxiety disorders she was vulnerable and began to consider self-harming again, and even suicide. She resisted the temptation because of her pregnancy but felt she was being pushed to the brink. I can't imagine what he was doing – she had no money or property. Was he just trying to manipulate her into committing suicide?

Talking to Jewel, I was reminded of the young nanny his other wife had told me about – the one Will Jordan had had an affair with, rejected, and then kept on the edge of sanity, saying one thing and doing another. When his wife had discovered the affair the nanny lost her job and was thrown out of her home. She left with nothing. She then came back later having taken an overdose of paracetamol. Even though she regretted taking the paracetamol and they got her to hospital, it was too late and she had multiple organ failure and died within a few days.

Will Jordan said he had watched her die, had held her hand and told her he cared and was with her to the end. He told Mischele about the incident on her hidden camera footage.

Mischele: 'It sounded like a horrible story . . .'

Will: 'It was. It was very unfortunate for everybody concerned. There was nobody who came out ahead, if you can call it that. There was nobody who got away from the emotional impact of that. And it was completely unintentional, which is what made it so much worse. Nobody really knew where her mind was. [Shrugs] You know . . . I certainly didn't. And I suppose, had I been a little less egocentric at that point I might have questioned things more than I did. But it didn't really go there. I never thought of it that way . . .

'I was there with her. You know, I was actually there with her, so in as much shock as the family and anybody else was. It was like "oh my gosh". Did I expect something? No, absolutely not. I mean it was only after the fact that we found out the background thing, what happened and so on, why she was . . .'

Mischele: 'Oh, I didn't get any of that. I only knew about what she had done.'

Will: 'That's cold. She had serious problems. Not blaming her family or anything like that but, you know, I know that shouldn't have a "favourite", but her sister was definitely the favourite. And she . . .' [he paused]

Mischele: '. . . was a neglected child?'

Will: 'Yeah, in a very bizarre kind of situation. And it was hard on her. Like I said, it is a sad story. I would have seen that, at least something, wasn't quite right instead of just seeing "cute girl throwing herself at you" and not really taking it any further than that. And I kick myself for behaving like that. Not because I made it happen but because, yeah, I did that. Especially because she was so much younger. And I think I failed abysmally, and . . .'

Mischele: 'How old were you then?'

Will: [pause/sighs] 'Thirty?'

Mischele: 'Oh, so young. It's been a long time.'

Will: 'Oh God, yeah.'

Mischele: 'I have no idea in terms of time frames of . . . anything.'

Will: 'And she was about twenty, or something.'

Mischele: 'So she was young!'

Will: 'Yeah, that is what made it all so bad . . . Um, and certainly from her perspective she didn't see anything wrong with what she was doing. She . . . had already kinda been getting chucked out of a situation so it was like, OK, so the storm can come through and nowhere to go so [shrugs]. You know, so . . . but there was more to it than that psychologically, and that is the bit that I just did not [gestures to head] . . .'

Mischele: '. . . get?'

Will: 'I didn't suspect it. I was totally clueless. I was just self-centred, self-absorbed and self-important.'

He explained how the nanny had been a very vulnerable and psychologically tortured young woman, rejected by her family (whose favourite was her sister). He said he was bowled over by her attentions but felt that he 'should have seen it' or at least known something wasn't quite right, instead of just seeing the 'cute girl' throwing herself at him. He admitted to kicking himself for behaving like that (for indulging in an affair, and letting her get caught by his wife and thrown out of his home). But then he regaled Mischele with the details of the nanny's death.

Will: 'It was horrible, it really was. That was an awful wake-up call. And of course there is nothing you can do about it. It wasn't even one of those kinda things that you can say, like, OK, you've got help in time. She was actually OK. I mean, you know, they pumped her stomach and whatever . . . but there was nothing to be done. She was dead, she was already a dead girl sitting. It was so cruel to see someone who is literally talking and everything else and sure she will be dead but it just took . . .'

Mischele: '. . . time.'

Will: 'So yeah, it was, it was awful and the only thing I could do was actually, at least, be there. I felt I owed her that. I got lots of crap from her family . . . which again, fair play, from their perspective they had reason to feel. And I am not going to sit there with a girl on her deathbed [and cause trouble] . . . It is easier to take it on the chin and let her last memories be good. Because she never had that.'

Mischele: 'But in their mind she was . . .'

Will: 'Yeah yeah, so I mean, it wasn't the time to try to [defend myself] . . . It would serve no difference.'

Mischele: 'It would've served no point.'

Will: 'Exactly. All it would do is . . . [gestures] If I could get used to that much, then maybe that was my role. Being able to replay some of the more . . . for . . . it was OK, it really was. But yeah, they went through the whole thing . . . you know. Some rather unpleasant things came out of that, and they found out themselves, everything was not all . . . [air quotes] but at least it didn't come from me, like I sat there and tried to throw darts . . . It came from the source.'

Mischele: '. . . Your wife.'

It was word salad again but the implication was that his wife had caused the problem by kicking the nanny out and then stirred up more trouble by telling the nanny's family about his affair with her.

I wondered if he was trying to replicate that experience with Jewel, testing and pushing her to see if he could make her commit suicide. If so, I wonder how many others he has done the same to. Maybe he just lost interest or was preoccupied with his father's situation, who by all accounts was showing signs of dementia.

Jewel struggled on with him, saying all the right things, but his actions were in complete contradiction to his words. In February 2019 she ended the relationship but carried on living with him until June 2019. She thought she needed to keep him involved in the pregnancy and had nowhere else to go. Things did not improve though and she finally moved out.

Jewel got in contact with me in July 2019 and was stunned to find that he had at least thirteen children already. She let me know when she went into labour and her little boy was born on 1 August 2019, my children's newest little brother (that I know of, anyway).

I know of at least two other women Will Jordan was involved with that overlap his relationship with Jewel.

On 1 September 2019 I got a message from Mischele stating that William Jordan had apparently stolen $10,000 from an employer called Lee – a second-hand car salesman and owner of a used car dealership. I contacted Lee and we spoke via video chat (something I always do with his victims in case it's Will Jordan trying to disguise his voice).

Shortly afterwards, we were contacted by Andrew, a landlord and another victim of Will Jordan. Along with Jewel's story it was possible to piece together the picture of what Will Jordan had been up to for the past year.

In 2018 Will Jordan's mother went into a home. Mischele told me she had found out that Will and his father had sold their family residence in the summer for a fairly decent amount of money and moved into rented accommodation. In January 2019, Will Jordan answered Andrew's advert on Facebook for a rental property above the offices to a car dealership. The landlord, Andrew, was swayed into believing that Will's father, John, was going to be living in the apartment on his own and would be helped out with the security deposit by the Navy Federal Credit Union.

Within a short space of time it was clear that not only was John living in the apartment but that Will Jordan and his girlfriend (Jewel) were also living there. Andrew confronted Will Jordan about it who readily agreed to sign an addendum adding him onto the lease.

The first month's rent was paid up front but the security deposit and further rent never materialised. There was excuse after excuse about delays in accessing the Navy Federal Credit Union funds, bounced cheques and faked bank wire confirmations, etc.

Will Jordan became friendly with the neighbour downstairs – a man called Lee who owned the car dealership – and offered to work in the office in return for pay and helping to set up and refine their computer systems and CCTV. He introduced them to his pregnant girl-friend Jewel who had come to live with him. Lee got to know her quite well. When Will began ducking her calls and ignoring her, Jewel would call Lee to see if Will was working so she could speak to him there. Lee was not impressed with Will Jordan's behaviour towards his pregnant girlfriend so he pulled him up on it. Will Jordan simply explained that he'd discovered the baby wasn't his and so he'd ended the relationship, saying she was just trying to get him back but he was having none of it.

Will Jordan then introduced Lee to another girl, Anna, who was blonde and about 5'4" tall. Anna told Lee that she was a fundraising expert, and so he asked Will and Anna to set up websites he had been thinking about to raise funds for hospitals in Cameroon as well as a website for his business.

In May 2019 Andrew served eviction notice on the family but it took another two months to get the Sheriff's department to finally lock them out of the apartment. In the meantime, Will Jordan was borrow-ing money from Lee to pay for the rent and food (rent that was never paid on to Andrew).

The car dealership website went live, as did the fundraising sites, but Lee said when he tried to access the funds raised there were none to be found. Also, the functionality of the car dealership website didn't work. Will Jordan said they were having some issues with the domain and that he would get it sorted. He was being evicted from the apartment and so stored some of his possessions in the office. Will Jordan even had his father stay overnight in the office before moving him on. Will Jordan sold his dad's car to Lee, but somehow lost the paperwork and although the $2,000 was paid for it, the car never materialised. Will Jordan had told Lee that he was a military veteran and was due money at the end of the month. When that didn't materialise either, Will told Lee that his father had cancer and he had to pay for chemotherapy instead. Further money went missing in the form of another $2,000 cheque, and then one of Lee's cars went missing too.

We are not sure what happened to Will Jordan's father. Some people were told that he has been put in a home, others that Will Jordan put his senile elder on a plane across country to Will's sister so that she could look after him. Either way, his father is no longer living with him.

In late July Will Jordan moved away to Vermont, seemingly to be with Anna. According to Lee he took with him $10,000 of money from the business as well as a car that did not belong to him. Lee has said that he is pressing charges but doesn't know where Will Jordan is now.

After Lee described Anna to me I showed him a picture of Rachel. He confirmed that it was the same person. So Rachel was seemingly still with him.

Whilst I was talking to Lee on video chat, Will Jordan telephoned him to explain that he 'had a past' and had some issues which they needed to discuss. He explained that he had just finished a job and had some cash for Lee which he would bring by the next day. Lee didn't believe him but found it interesting that he chose to call and explain things at that precise moment.

After that, Will Jordan would generally call him when someone was in the office with him or he was out. We suspect that Will Jordan was tapping into the CCTV or had bugged the office in order to ensure that he could keep the conversation going without having to actually speak to Lee, thereby preventing criminal charges being pressed. Will Jordan was constantly saying that he would come by imminently with money for Lee to repay him for everything.

Lee certainly said (repeatedly) that he had pressed charges but I don't think he actually did. I have my suspicions that as a second-hand car dealer he doesn't want to attract too much scrutiny.

◆　◆　◆

Shortly after Will Jordan disappeared from New Jersey – in the autumn of 2019 – I was contacted by a woman in Vermont. She had rented out half of her house to Will Jordan and Rachel. After Rachel's husband appeared at the landlady's door expecting to move in with his wife – this is someone who has repeatedly been told that she is not with Will Jordan any more – the landlady looked up Will Jordan's name and came across my website. She was frantic, particularly about the paedophile conviction, because she had two small children living with her at the property. I spoke to the landlady on video chat and she was determined to go to the police. After she had spoken to the local police, she rang me back, furious that they had refused to help. They said that Will Jordan had committed no crime against her yet and she would just have to try and evict them. She then told me she would talk to Will and Rachel later that afternoon and would get back to me after that.

She has not replied since. Although I have messaged her several times she has not answered and I suspect she has been sucked into his story that I am an enemy agent or something.

◆　◆　◆

I have said it before but it needs to be said again. Psychopaths never stop. They just learn new techniques or move onto new victims. Will Jordan will continue to do this. Even if put in prison again, he will continue to manipulate and control those around him, biding his time until he gets out and finds new victims to abuse. He will do this until the day he dies.

I am still trying to help people – still trying to educate potential victims of psychopaths and narcissists. Still trying to support their victims. Still trying to educate the public. It is only through knowledge, understanding and self-awareness that we will recognise and counteract toxic personalities. And the more of us who stand up to be counted and share our experiences without shame or embarrassment, the more that other people will feel empowered to do the same.

THE PRESENT

Because so much of what Will Jordan told me was lies, I recently decided to do a genetics DNA test on my children through ancestry. com. Will Jordan had claimed that he had Native American heritage as well as being partly Caribbean but even that was a lie. The resulting DNA heritage map of my two younger children was fascinating. They had European and Scottish heritage through me, and all-African through Will Jordan but nothing from any other continent. I am sure that in years to come more of my children's siblings will ask to be DNA tested and even get in touch with me and my family as that DNA connection will possibly answer some questions they may have.

My children have grown into strong and confident individuals. Robyn still has some anxiety but copes with it remarkably well. She has a full-time job now, and works as an illustrator and voice actor. She is pansexual which I initially didn't understand but now admire a lot. To be pansexual means that you are not solely attracted to same sex, or the opposite sex, or to trans people. In fact someone who is pansexual does not even think about someone's gender but instead is attracted to the person they are first and foremost. The genitals that an individual has are incidental to the relationship which develops. She is now engaged and in a very loving and stable relationship with a man whom she adores and who adores her.

My middle child, Eilidh, has already left school and is one of the most confident and fiery people I have ever met. She has a sharp brain, determination and a focus to achieve that far exceeds my own. In her first year at high school she got 100% on all her tests; it is obvious that she is very bright. One thing that Eilidh inherited was her father's aptitude for learning. At eight years old she watched *Dance Moms* and was inspired. She decided she was going to do the splits, so every day she stretched and practised until finally she was able to do the splits sideways as well as front to back. At fifteen she asked me if I could teach her a particular piece of music on the piano that I used to play. It was a piece from the film *The Piano* called *The Heart Asks Pleasure First*, which was a bit of a signature piece of mine. I laughed and said that I had passed my grade 8 piano before I had learnt to play that, and she had never played the piano at all. I told her she would need to learn the basics first and build up to it. Eilidh, being Eilidh, ignored me and decided to teach it to herself. Within two weeks she was playing it and two years later has a wide repertoire of pieces that she has taught herself. She put the same effort into taekwondo, winning medal after medal for patterns, sparring and high-jump kick. She got her black belt in 2018 and in 2019 she won the gold medal at the ITS British Championships.

Eilidh is also in a committed relationship with a bloke who is ideally suited to her. They seem to be perfectly matched and fit together really well – his cool to her fire.

Although I am not overly happy that both of my girls have met men who seem to be 'Mr Right' at such a young age, I think they are far better balanced than I ever was at their age. My life might have been very different if I had not 'played the field' and then stuck with the man I dated at eighteen! What I do know for certain is that they are strong, confident women who will stick up for themselves. If their relationships do not pan out, I know they will both survive and thrive in moving forward. In the meantime, they are enjoying their relationships and I wish them all the best. If their partners do not turn out to be 'Mr Right' then they are at least 'Mr Right Now'.

Over the last year my son has grown from a boy six inches shorter than me to a young man now taller than me. I am slightly grieving the loss of my little boy but am so proud of the man he is growing up to be. He is a loving and kind soul who aspires either to go to law school or to be a basketball star – or maybe both! He too got his black belt in taekwondo in 2018 and has won numerous medals for sparring and patterns over the years. He was also on the gold medal-winning Scottish team at the International ITS Championships in 2019.

I am immensely proud of all my children and their achievements. None of them have exhibited any issues with regards to their father, other than Robyn's anxiety which is as much to do with her own father as to do with her stepfather. My decision to be honest and open with them from the beginning appears to have been the right thing to do. It let them talk about the situation, ask questions and discuss what happened without any bitterness or anger. It allowed me to share with them what I learnt about his disorder to help them understand what they had experienced.

I decided to try dating again now that the children were older; I thought it would be interesting to explore the idea. I joined a dating app and put myself on the line again. I talked to a couple of people but mostly they were looking for 'sexting' or 'just a quickie', so they were quickly blocked. Then I started talking to a straightforward guy who seemed interested in an actual relationship. We agreed to meet for coffee and I thought long and hard about what to tell him about Will Jordan, my book and my career in talking about psychopaths. It's a hard one. I can imagine the conversation.

'So what do you do?'

'I'm an author.'

'Oh, really? What have you written?'

'A true crime memoir, called *The Bigamist*.'

That then spirals down into questions about the story and an explanation that my ex was a psychopathic con man who actively impregnates women to rip them off for money.

I have no embarrassment or difficulty in telling my story, however when it comes to dating there are two things that I imagine will happen. Firstly, if they find out before they get to know me, they might think that I am completely broken and an emotional wreck and so won't want to date me. Alternatively they might see that I am emotionally strong and secure, and then worry that if they mess up I might write a book about them and 'out' them to the world at large! If I don't tell them what really happened to me, I would have to think up some other story to tell them, and then isn't that lying? I play it down sometimes, and when people ask me the question 'So what do you do?', I tell them about the business I started and have built up over the past ten years. 'I am a publishing consultant, working with children and adults to help them become published authors.'

That takes us on a much lighter note and is fine for networking but feels only half true.

So when I was meeting this chap for a coffee date I decided I would tell him about the book and my experiences – but not immediately. I would see if I liked him first and decide later.

We met up for coffee in early February 2019 at a grand hotel. The lounge room was lovely – comfortable armchairs and autumn colours with a crackling fire in the fireplace. There was only us and one other couple on the other side of the room. He and I chatted for an hour or so, and it was very easy-going and comfortable. I rather liked him. He wasn't overly charming, seemed to be interested without being too intense.

Then something random happened.

As the other couple got up to leave, the woman came up to me and said, 'I recognise you – aren't you Mary Turner Thomson?'

'Yes,' I replied.

'I loved your book,' she said, '*The Bigamist*. I think you are an amazing woman. Such an ordeal to go through and you really opened my eyes to sociopaths. It helped me understand some of my past experiences.'

After I'd thanked her, she left quite quickly. I then turned back to my companion and realised by the quizzical look on his face that the choice whether to tell him or not had just been taken away from me. So I told him my story in brief. He seemed remarkably unconcerned and a bit disinterested by it (which was quite refreshing) and we carried on chatting about other things, including his telling me about his ex-wife and the trips they used to take on cruises, the motorbike he was buying and how proud he was of his grown-up son. We talked for three hours! At the end of the date he gave me a kiss on the cheek and asked for another date the next weekend. I decided to give it a go and said yes.

A few days later I got a horrible cold and was in bed for a couple of days. I texted back and forth and told him I was sick and had to cancel work for a few days and he seemed very sympathetic. On Valentine's Day, five days after our first date, he texted me a Valentine's card in the morning to which I responded. Then that evening, he texted me to say that he was 'calling an end to it' because I was not flirting enough and didn't seem interested in him. I have no idea where that came from and just messaged him back saying that was fine and 'just as a suggestion, maybe give the next girl a bit more time before coming to that conclusion, as a few days is really not enough time to gauge that.'

He texted me with comments making out that I was to blame for something and seemed to want me to argue or persuade him to change his mind. As far as I was concerned, it was done from the moment I read the words in his text.

I was perfectly pleasant to him (after all, we had only had one date and I was not emotionally involved yet). As far as I am concerned, I deserve someone who is prepared to put in a bit more effort than that. He got a bit nasty, accusing me of being unreachable, to which I replied, 'Well, next time it might be an idea to give a girl time to get to know you and even go on the second date before "calling an end to it" before either of you has had any time to explore "it".'

The next day he texted me with a cheerful note saying, 'How are you doing; what have you got on today?'

To which I simply replied, 'I thought you had called this to an end?'

He replied, 'Sorry.'

So I answered, 'For calling it to an end, or for texting this morning?'

He then just got belligerent, so I blocked him.

I am and have been quite happy on my own. I have occasionally wondered what it would be like to have a partner, and I would have loved my children to have a good father figure. There are some truly wonderful men out there, men who are supportive and loving, who do their share around the house, help shoulder the financial burden, and provide their partners with love. I just never met mine. I try not to dwell on why the man I believed was my 'soulmate' turned out to be a psychopath because it will not help anything. I still have dark days when I feel that the only (adult) person who truly loved me was my mother. However, most of the time I am positive and when I look at the practicalities of the situation I don't think I would like to share a bed with anyone again, nor have to wash another person's socks. So unless someone truly wonderful were to come along, I don't think I really want another relationship. I don't have time for 'settling' for someone just because they are there.

Over the years I have done something that I couldn't initially explain. I had a desire to speak to old boyfriends, to find out if any of the relationships I had had were real and whether I had indeed been loved at all. Not surprisingly, the people I contacted were surprised and confused to hear from me and were usually rather dismissive. I must admit that it must have been a bit strange my calling them out of the blue. Then one day my sister mentioned that she had bumped into one of my first boyfriends from when I was nineteen years old. He had not only been a boyfriend but a mutual first love, and although the initial relationship had only lasted about a year we had remained friends for more than a decade after, before life got in the way and we drifted apart.

I called him out of the blue and his reaction blew me away. He was happy to hear from me and devastated to hear what had happened. He called me back the next day, angry and needing to talk about it, saying 'how dare' anyone treat his Mary like that. I was so touched. I had always loved him and it made me feel like I had something to hold on to.

It meant everything to me that at least one of my relationships had been real, at least one man had loved me enough to still care years later. We rekindled our friendship although we rarely see each other. He has a partner and a child now so there is no romance, but it helps me to know that there could have been.

LIFE MOVES ON

At the end of my relationship with Will Jordan I had to deal with the worst experience of my life, losing my mother. In some ways this pushed me rudely into full adulthood at the ripe age of forty-one. My father, although a decent man, was a very old-fashioned gentleman. He earned the money to support the family and did all the 'dad' stuff like DIY around the house, looking after the garden and the like, but was never very involved with us as children. He was there but did his own thing. However, he was an infinitely better father than Will Jordan was to my children. One of my favourite memories of my dad as a child was him getting a dark green MG two-seater sports car, when I was maybe four or five years old, and him letting me sit on his lap and steer whilst he took the controls – something that would be totally illegal today. I suppose it is such a special memory for me because it was exciting and different, but also because I was getting my father's undivided attention. A rare occasion indeed for the youngest of his four children.

When my mother died, my father did his best to step up and be a good parent to us all. Although we were already well into adulthood it was really the first time that I got to know him as a person rather than a shadowy father figure. When he was eighty-five his conversation started to get a bit circular, so I started to work with him to write down his own life story which was fascinating. Born in 1925, he had seen so much change in the world. He could remember being aged ten and going down George Street in Edinburgh in his grandfather Fred's horse and carriage, with the dogs running along between the back wheels. A policeman (there were no traffic lights in Edinburgh at that time) held up his hand to tell Fred to stop and Fred just waved back as if the policeman was being friendly. My father was impressed that Fred had got away with it! Dad's school was bombed during the Second World War, killing the headmaster, and when he was old enough he left for officer training in the Navy. At the end of his training he was deployed to his ship and the moment he arrived was told to stow his stuff because they were off! When he asked where they were going, he was told, 'It's D-Day!' His ship was laying down smoke in the English Channel to mask the movement of the troop ships, so they had to go back and forth the whole time whilst being shelled.

Dad was given a cine-camera and asked to film the action. At the time he thought it was a very important job, but later when he asked who he should give the film to and was told to keep it, he realised that the camera had just ensured that he kept out of the way. It did, however, give him an interest, and after the war (and a degree in maths from Cambridge, as well as a brief stint in publishing and teaching) he entered the new emerging industry of television in 1950. After that he rode the rising tide of television until he retired at fifty-five and then did some freelance video production work.

It was interesting having a father in television. He and my mother had fascinating friends, often people who were quite famous. Whenever we went to see a play, my father would suggest that we go backstage and say hello to the cast, something I thought was quite normal but apparently not! The cast always seemed to be delighted to see us, especially when Dad mentioned he was a TV producer.

After my mother died, my dad sold the family home and moved into a very nice flat where he stayed for twelve years. He did get a bit forgetful but after writing his life story it seemed to completely reignite his brain. However, in the process of writing this book that you are reading, in January 2018, my father became ill. Just two months short of his ninety-third birthday, he initially seemed a little confused, so I did a dementia test on him. I asked him to say the months of the year in reverse order. 'OK,' he said, 'December, November, October, Spain . . .' and then stopped. He knew he'd got it wrong but didn't know in what way. We tried to get him help to be assessed but things went downhill very fast and a few days later he woke up asking whose flat he was in. My sister and I did our best to look after him at home with almost round-the-clock care, but within a couple of weeks it was clear that he was declining fast.

He seemed physically all right, albeit rather confused, and he had a few falls. He started to hallucinate from time to time. He would point at the blank wall and ask, 'Who's that boy?' or 'Who's that woman standing there?' They seemed to be just shadows and images. He was not delusional though, and when we explained there was nothing there he would accept that he was hallucinating. It became clear what was happening one day when he pointed to the floor and said:

'What are those people doing down there?'

I asked, 'Are they small people, Dad?'

'No,' he said, confused by the question, 'they're normal-sized people.'

'Who are they?' I asked.

'They're doctors,' he said.

'What do you think they're doing then?'

'Well' – he paused – 'they're being doctors!'

Suddenly I knew what was going on. My father had started the first ever TV medical drama in the 1950s, a show called *Emergency Ward 10*. It was filmed in a massive ATV/ITV studio and as the producer he had worked in a glass-fronted editing suite on the second floor overlooking all the studio scenes. I had seen pictures of the view showing the actors dressed as doctors, shot from high above. What my father was experiencing was 'end-of-life delirium'. His brain was shutting down and rather than have his life 'flash' before his eyes, it was happening slowly over an extended period of time. In some ways it was like people from his past were coming to say goodbye. His childhood friends, his mother, his wife, his work colleagues. He was not distressed by it at all and I think even found comfort in it.

Finally he grew very cold and confused, so I called an ambulance and he was taken to hospital. He was only aware he was there for the first couple of days before the confusion finally took over. He died within a week.

Although I was sad to lose my father, I truly feel that he had lived a full life. He was an incredibly lucky man, always landing on his feet, no matter what life threw at him. Up until this sudden illness he was happily living in his own home and having quite a comfortable existence. However, I think he was ready to go whereas my mother died at seventy-seven and there was so much more she would have done.

Sorting out my father's estate was traumatic, not least because when we put my father's flat on the market we got an immediate offer from a chap who came to see it. We were told that everything was sorted out and the deal was done, so we cleared the place and cleaned every inch. The day before the chap was due to move in though, he announced that he had not yet got his mortgage sorted and it would be another few weeks before he could move. The weeks went by and it was excuse after excuse as to why things were delayed. His broker had let him down so he had gone directly to the bank; they had lost some paperwork so he was going to another bank, etc.

I was strongly reminded of Will Jordan's excuses and found the whole experience incredibly stressful. Within the first week of excuses I was warning my siblings that this was not right but there was nothing we could do about it. Finally, after two months of daily delays, we put the flat back on the market and told the chap he could bid for it again if he wanted. We got a better offer the second time and took great pleasure in telling the man to get lost. I have no idea what he was getting from the experience other than to mess us around. Possibly another psychopath, or maybe he was just delusional and aiming for something he simply did not have capacity to achieve.

So finally it was all sorted out. My share of the inheritance meant that I had enough capital to finally get back on the property market myself, and with a mortgage I managed to buy a house almost a year after my father died. It is not a glamorous dwelling and not in the most salubrious area – in fact it is rather small and filled to the gunnels – but it is *my* house. For months I went around touching the walls and saying, 'These are *my* walls' and 'This is *my* floor', with an overwhelming feeling of happiness and contentment. Having spent twelve years renting flats and having to move every time a landlord decided they wanted to have their sister move in, or that they were going to sell up, *finally* having my own home again was (and still is) incredible. Mentally getting back what I had lost and feeling that I am in control of my own home environment is wonderful. If I want to paint the walls, I can. If I want to pull down the shed or dig up the garden, I can. It is mine and that feels very good.

New Beginnings

I have gone through every aspect of my life over the past thirteen years – reclaiming each part, emotionally, mentally, physically, financially, professionally and spiritually. I went over each area of my life and revisited places I had been to with Will Jordan, but this time on my own or with other people. I went to see theatre productions we had seen together on my own again or with friends. When I was in London for some media interviews I went to the theatre where *Les Misérables* was being performed and explained to the ticket office why I was there. They gave me a very expensive seat for a fraction of the price and I sat and cried through the whole thing. I am not sure the man who was sitting next to me was best pleased as I sniffed my way through it. I also went back to see *Phantom of the Opera* on my own and visited the restaurants we had been to together. I rewatched movies and listened to songs we had shared, this time with new feelings and taking new meanings from the words. I revisited the flat in Portobello, and the house in Dick Place. I didn't go into either but made my peace with both. I sat in cafés where I had met Will Jordan and treated myself to a lovely coffee as I sat and read a book or played a game, thinking about anything other than him. Gradually I removed Will Jordan from my life.

I got rid of everything he had touched in my home, replaced furniture over time and removed things he had bought. I gave everything of his to a charity shop and sold my wedding ring and bought something very mundane with the proceeds – I don't even remember what now. Anything that reminded me of him was removed or relived without him.

I healed the emotional scars by making new memories and moving forward.

The last time I self-harmed was one isolated incident in 2004 when I was with Will Jordan. It was whilst I was awake in the middle of the night, having heard noises and believing that the 'unsavouries' Will Jordan had told me about had come to kidnap my children. I had already searched the house in a terrified panic and then sat down at the kitchen table, still holding the illegal taser that Will Jordan had trained me how to use. I was in such a state of stress that I took a carving knife and painstakingly slowly – and very deliberately – cut down the top of my left inner forearm. It was nowhere near the arteries and was not a suicide attempt, just a physical manifestation of the emotional pain I was in. It helped distract from the stress I was in at the time but it left a long silvery scar.

Every time I see that scar, I am reminded of everything that Will Jordan put me through. I am reminded of how I allowed myself to be placed in that position and how close I felt to losing my mind. Finally I decided that I didn't want to be taken back to that angst any longer. So in January 2019 I got my first tattoo. It is a colourful writer's quill, almost the whole length of my inner forearm, which has just penned an infinity symbol. Coming out of the feather are three birds taking flight.

It's a huge motivator for me and encompasses the three things I am most proud of in this life. When I look at my arm now, instead of seeing the pain I cut into, I see my writing and what my book has achieved in the feathered quill; I see my black belt in the infinity symbol; and I see my three children taking flight. Very soon I plan to add to that tattoo with other birds that morph into books, and books that change into birds, to represent all the children I have worked with writing stories as well as all the people my book has helped.

So finally I am back on my feet. I have my own home, my own business, and my family, whilst my life is getting better all the time. My children are all living at home for the time being and I love having them around, even if it is a bit crowded and chaotic. They won't be living here forever so I will just enjoy them whilst I have them.

This is not the end. This is just the end of one chapter in my life. What the rest of the 'book' holds I don't really know. I do know that it's not the last I will hear of Will Jordan. I know that he won't stop, that he will never stop. I will hear from new victims and other children. From other people whose lives he's financially ruined or emotionally destroyed. I know that there is a whole new generation yet to come as well.

I also know that I will continue to help people. I will continue to hear their stories about how they've had experiences with psychopaths, sociopaths and narcissists. How people have been used and abused to the point they don't know how to stand up again. I hope that my story will help them recover. I want to be able to inspire people not to feel embarrassed or ashamed of what's happened to them. I hope I can show them that you do not have to be destroyed by an experience like this. That it does take time, patience and a good deal of self-control, but that it is possible. To get back on top. To let go of the past. To forgive yourself for being naive or gullible or simply for being kind. And to be able to move on with life in a positive, strong and happy way.

I am very pleased and extremely proud that I was able to write a book about this, and that I was able to share my story and create so many opportunities from it. Writing it all down is still the most cathartic thing I have ever done. And I think it helps so many other people when they are able to read it. I cannot say how much it means to me when I read messages and comments on my Facebook page or reviews of the book on Amazon (and yes, I do read each and every one) saying that my story and my book has helped them better understand their own experience and allowed them to view it all in a new light. It means my experience was not wasted and has some value in this world. It also shows all the other people going through something similar that they are indeed *not* alone!

Thank you for reading my story. Thank you for being the audience that made my story worthwhile. Good luck and I hope something wonderful happens to you today.

Mary x

APPENDIX: A BRIEF GUIDE TO SPOTTING AND COMBATTING TOXIC TECHNIQUES

There are some truly fascinating research reports done on the language and techniques that psychopaths use to manipulate their targets and people around them. One of these is *Hungry like the wolf: A word-pattern analysis of the language of psychopaths*. In 2011, Dr Jeffrey Hancock of Cornell University and now a professor of communication in Stanford's School of Humanities and Sciences and founding director of the Stanford Social Media Lab, teamed up with Dr Michael Woodworth, a professor of psychology from the University of British Columbia in Canada. Dr Woodworth was researching psychopathic and non-psychopathic murderers in criminal facilities whilst Dr Hancock was researching language. Using computerised text analysis, Woodworth and Hancock found that psychopathic criminals tend to make identifiable word choices when talking about their crimes.

Dr Woodworth interviewed eighteen psychopaths (as identified through the PCL-R), as well as thirty-eight non-psychopathic killers in criminal facilities throughout Canada.

They discovered that psychopaths were more likely to talk about their crime in terms of being instrumental. In other words, the psychopaths committed their crimes in order to accomplish a particular aim, whereas non-psychopaths tended to commit their crimes in a reactionary way, such as killing a lover after discovering they had been unfaithful. When talking about their crimes the psychopaths used darker language and referenced their crimes as being further in the past as if they had distanced themselves more from their actions. The psychopaths also talked far more about their basic needs during the crimes. They noted what they had eaten that day, what they had drunk, the money they had gained, whereas non-psychopathic killers tended to concentrate on other subjects like religion, spirituality and family.

Dr Hancock surmised that on Maslow's 'Hierarchy of Needs' psychopaths are more interested in a lower level of basic needs than empathic people, that is food, water, money, shelter, than the higher-level needs of family, self-esteem and self-actualisation. This might be because psychopaths already have an internal grandiose ideal of who they are and therefore don't need to think about it, but instead are interested in their material needs. It was the psychopaths' interest in talking about what they had eaten on the day they killed someone that gave the report its title, *Hungry like the wolf.*

Woodworth stated, 'You can spend two or three hours with a psychopath and come out feeling hypnotised.' The level of body language and distraction they use is key here, as well as the fact that they use this technique to distract people from the underlying message. They are so good at manipulating people face to face it is disturbing, even for qualified research specialists.

So although their language is quite distinct, their face-to-face and non-verbal communication is really the way they manipulate individuals.

Research to determine whether you can analyse language within social media to identify psychopaths in the community could be vital as everything we do digitally leaves a record of the way we speak or write.

One way to apply this research would be to see if you can identify psychopaths through the language they use on social and digital media, then clinicians and investigators could better understand the motivations of their subjects. Obviously this cannot be used as 'stand-alone' evidence but it can support the investigators' or clinicians' other evidence. For instance, if written and digital media can highlight potential for psychopathy then law enforcement personnel would be likely to interview their suspect in a different way, for instance possibly using non-humans to interview them in the future. Rather like a polygraph, this is not currently admissible as evidence in court.

When it comes to online dating, Hancock has worked with a friend who had an online dating company in the UK. The company had a small team of people trained to identify problematic profiles, such as people who had been reported as being violent, and the team would then 'ghost' the profile. That is when the online dating company makes that profile invisible to everyone else but the profile owner, who thinks they are on the site although no one can actually see them. I thoroughly approve of that because if the profile were just kicked off the site they would simply move onto another dating site, and I believe and know that delaying psychopaths can save victims. As there are now around 8,000 dating sites and millions of online dating profiles, it would need automated language analysis service to identify them.

Of course, this may become possible in the future, although not now, but it is good to know that people are looking into this.

However, there are techniques that we know toxic people use to manipulate and control others. I thought it useful to list the techniques that psychopaths, narcissists and sociopaths use to manipulate people, and more specifically how to counteract them.

Love-Bombing

'Love-bombing' is a technique that toxic people use to suck their victims in, get under their defences and firmly get their hooks in. It breaks down their victim's resistance and programmes them to be compliant. It starts with compliments and public displays of affection, as well as lavish gifts. Basically everything that someone might want from a blossoming romance, and the sort of things we have all seen in romantic movies as the couple are swept off their feet and fall in love. Most addictive of all are the promises for a better future. These people (sometime covertly) find out their target's desires and goals and make promises that far exceed their expectations, encouraging them to think bigger and further outside their comfort zone, thereby pulling their victim off balance whilst also believing that this new partner only had their best interests at heart.

They will refer to being 'soulmates' and declare undying love within a few weeks of meeting and generally it feels like they are pulling the relationship forward a little too fast, but the target goes with it to see where it leads.

The toxic person is affectionate and loving, and they seem totally focused on their mark. Things progress quickly and the victim ends up feeling like this is what they've been missing in every other relationship they have ever had.

It is conditioning. It is grooming.

As soon as they are hooked solidly, things will start to change.

Pretty soon the demonstrations of love will only happen when the victim behaves and does what the toxic person wants. It becomes selective and deliberately manipulative.

It is difficult to spot 'love-bombing' because it looks like a genuine relationship. All new relationships are exciting and the promise of a future together is intoxicating. Getting to know someone new gives emotional highs and alarm bells are not usually ringing! The key to spotting 'love-bombing' is the speed at which it happens. The toxic person will demand a lot of your time, and social media makes it easy, with texts, messaging, posting, etc., as well as long telephone calls and dates. We make it very easy for these toxic people to be in constant contact with us and they take advantage of it. The toxic person doesn't want you to stop and think about what's happening . . . Remember, they want to sweep you off your feet so that you cannot rationalise what happens later.

Toxic people often target previous victims of trauma. I don't think this is particularly sadistic, just that victims of trauma (who have recovered and come to terms with that trauma) often overlook or explain away the flaws in others. They have empathy for a 'damaged' person and toxic people use that to explain away any negative traits.

Love-bombing prepares the way for everything else. It puts the victim into a fog which will only ever properly lift once the victim is out of that situation.

How to protect yourself:

- Go slow – anyone worth being with will respect that!
- Set boundaries – if you feel pressured by them, that is a red flag.
- Don't get too wrapped up in the moment.
- Don't be overly empathetic, try to fix people, or share too much of yourself early on. It's important in a genuine relationship to actually get to know someone but keep something in reserve that's just for you!

Gaslighting

This term was coined after the 1944 film *Gaslight*, in which the husband purposefully makes his wife think she is going mad, in order to hide his criminal activity.

Gaslighting is a deliberate attempt to sow the seeds of doubt in victims' minds (either an individual or a group). It makes victims doubt their own memory or perception of reality, and even to question their own sanity. The toxic person uses lying, misdirection, contradiction and denial with such confidence and conviction that the victim – who has been love-bombed already and believes the toxic person has only their best interests at heart – feels the problem must lie within.

The toxic person uses statements like:

'That didn't happen.'

'You imagined it!'

'Are you crazy?'

'Fake news!'

It's an insidious manipulative tactic and distorts and erodes the victim's sense of reality. It eats away at self-trust and disables the justification for calling out abuse and mistreatment.

The toxic person convinces the victim that trusting their own experience is a sign of dysfunction and that the only person they can truly trust is the abuser. To the victim the ground is always shifting and whenever they get a grasp of the situation it changes. Especially after being love-bombed, the gaslighting period is very painful. The victim just wants (and craves) to get back the lovely person their partner was before, and how special they made them feel. They have bought into the dreams and ideals that the love-bomber sold them, and so trust that this is just a 'rocky patch' that they will get through eventually. Meanwhile, the victim succumbs and imperceptibly shrinks into themselves day by day, allowing the gaslighter to take full control.

How to protect yourself:

- Ground yourself in reality.
- Don't let things 'slide' or become distracted from your own reality.

- Write things down as they happen so you can refer back to it later. Writing is a powerful tool to sort out your thoughts. Putting things down on paper gives you a distance and perspective that you cannot get from just thinking alone.
- Talk to friends and your support network. The power of a validating community can reground a distorted reality from a malignant person and back to inner trust. Also, be very wary of a partner who tries to drive a wedge between you and your other relationships (such as friends and family)! Keep lines of communication open.
- Be centred in your own reality.
- Validate your own identity. Take time for yourself to ensure you are grounded, do mindfulness exercises and journal your feelings.

Projection and Reframing

This is when the toxic person turns any flaw or situation around to blame someone else for something they have done and make it look like they are the victim. For instance, this might be accusing their victim of lying when it is they who have told the lie. A classic example of this is an unfaithful partner accusing their spouse of cheating. It is a way of avoiding ownership of a situation or any accountability. Emotionally damaged people can do this unconsciously, but toxic people tend to do it deliberately. Rather than acknowledge their own flaws or imperfections, a toxic person will outrageously dump their own traits on their victims, which can be painful and cruel: accusing their partners of cheating, lying, stealing, being selfish, unkind, thoughtless, cruel, ignoring them, disinterested, etc.

Another form of this is sometimes called 'reframing', where the toxic person changes your legitimate experience into supposed character flaws and evidence of irrationality.

Reframing is a technique used in therapy to help create a different way of looking at a scenario, situation, person or relationship – simply by changing its meaning. It is a strategy that therapists use to help clients look at their situation from a different perspective and adjust thought patterns, leaving the client feeling healthier and more in control. However, it can also be used by toxic people to change how their victim views something they themselves have done.

For instance, after a victim simply expresses feelings that the toxic person has been rude to the victim, the toxic person might state:

'Oh, so now you're perfect?' or 'So I'm a bad person, huh?'

It is a pre-emptive defence because they are putting dramatic words in their victims' mouths, deliberately invalidating the victim's right to have thoughts and emotions about inappropriate behaviour. Plus it is designed to instil a sense of guilt when trying to establish boundaries, by accusing the victim of being unkind or having toxic thoughts before the victim has even had a chance to discuss the issue with the perpetrator.

It can be incredibly frustrating to deal with 'projection' or 'reframing'. They are gaslighting techniques and leave the victim feeling 'Is it me?' A good example of this is being accused of being selfish because the victim takes time for themselves away from the toxic person and their family responsibilities. This leaves the victim feeling defensive and cautious around the projector, like walking on eggshells.

How to protect yourself:

- Try to avoid getting sucked in. It's good to be open to constructive criticism but you need to take a step back and ask, 'Is that really about me?'
- Again, write it down, and look back at it a bit later. Does it sound like it makes sense?
- Don't 'project' your empathy onto others, and don't 'own' other people's faults.

- If someone tries to put words in your mouth (such as 'So I'm a bad person now, huh?'), just reply, 'I never said that' and walk away. Set firm boundaries by not engaging in this type of interaction.

Nonsensical Conversation/Word Salad

Word salad, or nonsensical conversation, does happen naturally within psychiatry. People with psychiatric disorders (such as dementia or schizophrenia) can unconsciously produce a string of words that don't make sense, although they often think that they do. However, toxic people can consciously use this as a technique to baffle, confuse or off-balance their victim. The idea is to disorientate their victim and get them off track (especially if challenging them in any way). It ensures that the victim doesn't have a satisfactory resolution to a conversation and so gives up asking the difficult questions. The victim is left trying to work out what was just said, so instead of moving on to their next point it disrupts their internal thought process. In the end the victim is left wondering what the whole argument was about in the first place. The toxic person will include projection, blame-shifting, sympathy ploys, stonewalling, bringing up unrelated issues, and starting the conversation over and over again. It is consciously done to discredit, confuse, frustrate and distract from the main purpose.

For instance, it might start with the victim bringing a concern or question to the toxic person. Firstly there is either no straight answer, or a lie. If the victim continues to request an answer, the toxic person will escalate the conversation using multiple forms of distraction or deflection, or even tell you it is not a topic they will discuss. They might say something inflammatory and start an argument about a different topic, such as accusing the victim of distrust or infidelity. When the victim defends themselves or asks the toxic person to stop, the toxic person will use that as proof that they are indeed guilty.

The key is for the toxic person to avoid answering the rational questions or allowing their victim to have any satisfying resolution. It is baffling for the victim and leaves them completely off balance. One example of this is very simple: when asked why the toxic person did something (or didn't do it) they may just reply, 'I'm not going to argue with you.' If the victim persists, they are accused of 'not letting it go' or leaving the victim feeling blamed for causing drama, and the behaviour itself remains unaddressed.

Meanwhile the toxic person will continue to reward and love-bomb again, so that when the subject is dropped and the victim backs down, the toxic person will remind the victim how much they are loved and forgive them for nagging, or causing a scene.

You can tell that you are in a nonsensical conversation if you find:

- The conversation appears to be circular, points you make seem to be totally disregarded and the toxic person goes over their points again and again, getting nowhere.
- If you bring up bad behaviour they will be reminded of a past wrongdoing, causing distraction and putting you on the defensive.
- The toxic person talks in a condescending or patronising tone – they will stay calm but you will become increasingly confused as the conversation becomes more and more irrational. The toxic person uses your reactions against you saying that you are 'out of control'.
- You find that suddenly you appear to be defending yourself for the very behaviour that you were criticising in them – this is reversal of blame, as they are projecting their bad behaviour onto you.
- The toxic person changes tactics mid-conversation, showing a variety of personas – anger, insults, tenderness, 'poor

me', or being conciliatory. They are just trying to find a tactic that works.

- You find yourself having to start explaining basic human emotions (such as why you are hurt by an action or inaction) as well as the normal expectancy of a relationship (such as respect and honesty).

- Without accepting responsibility they will find excuses for their behaviour (youth, abuse, alcohol, lack of attention), something that if it works they will refer to again and again without making any steps to address the issue or change the behaviour.

- Every time you make a valid point, they counter with long monologues that change the subject, meander and misdirect, arguments that knock you sideways and take your thought processes down a completely new avenue.

- You get blanket statements like 'I don't want to argue', 'You are never satisfied' or 'You're always too sensitive', especially if the discussion was not an argument.

The toxic person will use words against the victim in a circular tactic, which both manages to confuse and convince the victim that they are at fault. It is done consciously and is designed to distract, punish or demean the victim until they give up and accept the toxic person's version of events. What's more, the victim is completely unaware that this is happening because they are being gaslit to believe their lack of understanding is down to their own incompetence.

Over time the toxic person 'trains' their victim to simply accept their version of reality. In the process the victim is left emotionally exhausted and vulnerable, nervous about saying anything at all in case they are found to be at fault, and aware that nothing will be resolved even if they do.

Sometimes, in trying to rationalise the toxic person's words, the victim will toggle together something that makes sense, generally in a positive way. So they make up the toxic person's excuse for them, one that works for the victim.

For instance, when faced with overwhelming proof that he was married to someone else, Will Jordan said, 'All I will say is that she is all about money.' Had I still been under his control I might well have taken that to mean that the other wife was blackmailing him, or that he had married her to stay in the UK and paid her for the privilege, or alternatively that she was being paid by someone else to say those things. As it was, I knew the truth and did not fall into his carefully worded trap.

In normal conversation, two people try to align their realities and to see each other's point of view. The toxic person has a completely different agenda. They want to assert their dominance and superiority, so it suits their interests not to lay any groundwork at all. For instance, if wanting to ask why they didn't turn up for a date, the toxic person might assert that the date was not really fixed or confirmed or was never discussed in the first place, before distracting with asking if the victim has had a bad day and that's why they're being so hostile.

How to protect yourself:

- Know the signs of a nonsensical conversation and pay attention to how they make you feel over time.
- If you feel that you can't open your mouth and say exactly what you think in a relationship, then there is a problem.
- Before you approach a person to discuss an issue, write down what it is you want to find out. After the conversation, go back to what you wrote and see if you got an answer that satisfied you.
- Don't continue to feed them a supply of points. Rather, focus on one issue and keep going back to it.

- Resist generalised statements (such as 'I don't want to argue' or 'You're never satisfied' or 'You're too sensitive') by not taking the bait. Say, 'I'm not arguing either, I just want to know . . .' or 'Well, I'm not satisfied in this instance,' and ask the question again. Or say, 'Well, I'm sensitive about this subject, and I want to know . . .'

Knowing and understanding the control dramas and toxic techniques helps victims to recognise when they're being manipulated. That awareness in itself stops toxic techniques from working.

I had a long conversation with a friend in 2019 who was in a toxic relationship. I talked her through the techniques and control dramas, which she recognised and identified with. However, she was still resisting. She said that if she stood up to her toxic partner he might leave, which left her feeling powerless. The truth is that you cannot thrive in any kind of relationship that keeps you cowed and under control, even if they're not psychopathic in nature. People should be able to relax and say what they think, and at the same time feel that their partner supports and loves them. If that is not happening, then it might not the right relationship.

FURTHER READING/VIEWING

Books

Simon Baron-Cohen, *Zero Degrees of Empathy: A New Theory of Human Cruelty* (Penguin, 2011)

Sandra L. Brown, *Women Who Love Psychopaths: Inside the Relationships of Inevitable Harm with Psychopaths, Sociopaths, & Narcissists* (Mask Publishing, 2010)

Robert D. Hare, *Without Conscience: The Disturbing World of the Psychopaths Among Us* (The Guilford Press, 1999)

Liane J. Leedom, *Just Like His Father?* (Healing Arts Press, 2006)

Reid J. Meloy, *The Psychopathic Mind: Origins, Dynamics, and Treatment* (Rowman & Littlefield, 2004)

Jon Ronson, *The Psychopath Test* (Picador, 2012)

Alice Sebold, *Lucky* (Picador, 2003)

Sarah Smith, *Deceived: A True Story* (Orion, 2007)

Martha Stout, *The Sociopath Next Door: The Ruthless versus the Rest of Us* (Broadway Books, 2006)

Web Links (articles and videos)

Psychopathy:

Hungry like the wolf: A word-pattern analysis of the language of psychopaths by Jeffrey T. Hancock, Michael T. Woodworth and Stephen Porter: www.youtube.com/watch?reload=9&v=6vF5PtdiiCo

Article about Dr Robert Hare and his PCL-R: www.discovermagazine.com/mind/into-the-mind-of-a-psychopath

I am <fishead(– a film about psychopaths in the workplace. The introduction to this documentary left me almost in a state of panic attack. I listened to it over and over again, feeling like I was being punched in the gut. The documentary is well worth a watch and explains very clearly how psychopaths operate in the workplace. www.filmsforaction.org/watch/i-am-fishead-2011/

Psychology Today article on sex and the psychopath: www.psychologytoday.com/gb/blog/insight-is-2020/201410/sex-and-the-psychopath

'Did He Ever Love Me? A Study of Life With a Psychopathic Husband' qualitative report: www.civicresearchinstitute.com/online/article_abstract.php?pid=6&iid=592&aid=4305

Spectrum of psychopathy: https://lovefraud.com/experienced-clinician-says-psychopathy-is-a-spectrum/

LoveFraud article about Will Jordan: https://lovefraud.com/true-lovefraud-stories/will-allen-jordan/

Donald Trump's language style: https://news.liverpool.ac.uk/2018/01/19/one-year-trump-linguistics-expert-analyses-us-presidents-influence-language/

Psychopathic Traits and Perceptions of Victim Vulnerability by S. Wheeler: https://journals.sagepub.com/doi/abs/10.1177/0093854809333958

Jon Ronson:

You can listen to the *Internet Date from Hell* radio programme with Jon Ronson here: www.youtube.com/watch?v=oXsorUZMhdQ

The *Guardian* article where Jon mentions having written *The Psychopath Test* after our interview: www.theguardian.com/books/2012/jan/03/jon-ronson-psychopath-test-paperback-qna

Review of *The Psychopath Night*: www.yorkpress.co.uk/leisure/comedy/14905389.review-jon-ronson-psychopath-night-central-methodist-church-york-november-11

Online support and information for victims:

www.lovefraud.com – website for victims of sociopaths and psychopaths

www.ncbi.nlm.nih.gov/pubmed/23422847 – 'Psychopathy and Victim Selection: The Use of Gait as a Cue to Vulnerability' by Brock University, Ontario.

Empathy:

www.psychologytoday.com/us/blog/tech-support/201701/6-things-you-need-know-about-empathy

https://highlysensitiverefuge.com/empath-signs/

www.independent.co.uk/life-style/empath-signs-filters-boundaries-solitary-nature-character-narcissism-psychology-personality-a8165701.html

https://happyproject.in/empathy-hurts/

www.sheknows.com/health-and-wellness/articles/1096279/traits-that-make-you-susceptible-to-a-psychopath/

Information for parents/carers:

www.barnardos.org.uk/what-we-do/helping-families/children-with-a-parent-in-prison – information for supporting children with a parent in jail

www.nicco.org.uk – UK national information centre for supporting children of offenders

ABOUT THE AUTHOR

Photo © 2020 Mary Turner Thomson

Mary Turner Thomson grew up in Edinburgh. She has a BA Hons in Creative and Performing Arts, as well as diplomas in marketing, business advice and literature/creative writing. She worked as a business adviser, marketing consultant and motivational trainer before deciding to write *The Bigamist*, a memoir of her marriage to a con man and bigamist.

Mary is also the co-author of *Trading Places* (2009), the true story of how Natalie Hutchison suffered domestic abuse but took her life back by starting her own business, even winning the Trading Places award in 2006. She has also written a comedic book about what sociopaths say and what they really mean in *The Sociopath Subtext*.

Mary is currently working on her first novel, a psychological thriller.

If you want to find out more, sign up to Mary's website or follow her on Facebook and/or Twitter:

Website: **www.maryturnerthomson.com**

Facebook: **maryturnerthomson**

Twitter: **@TheBigamistBook**